I Am Bunny

How a "Talking" Dog Taught Me Everything
I Need to Know About Being Human

Alexis Devine

WILLIAM MORROW

An Imprint of HarperCollinsPublishers

HarperCollins books may be purchased for educational, business, or sales promotional use. For information, please email the Special Markets Department at SPsales @harpercollins.com.

Illustrations on pages 21, 44, 58, 79, 106, 126, 154, 173, 197, 226 © 2023 by Agata Zlotko.

Photographs on pages i, ii, ix, 93, 103, 118, 141, 158, 191, 195, 230, 256, 259 © 2023 by Rhiannon Brunett, Thisisrhi Photography.

Photographs on pages 16, 24, 26, 37, 49, 62, 77, 84, 97, 110, 135, 170, 205, 214, 215, 222, 234 © 2023 by Elle Hanley.

Photographs on pages 7, 11, 32, 35, 70, 74, 221, 224, 237, 238, 243 © 2023 by Vera Pashkevich/Vera Pash Photo.

Photographs on pages x, 53, 67, 114, 123, 130, 145, 150, 176, 179, 184, 201, 211, 250, 252, 255 © 2023 by Amanda Calquhoun.

Photographs on pages 43, 57, 69, 101, 213 © 2023 by Lance Reis.

Photographs on page 203 courtesy of Nicole Wyatt.

Photograph on page 5 courtesy of Julie Kane.

Photographs on pages xii, 2, 18, 27, 39, 50, 54, 56, 64, 88, 137, 139, 167, 209, 217, 218, 219, 223, 239, 241, 247 courtesy of the author.

Illustrations on pages i, 141, 230 ©MicroOne/stock.adobe.com

Illustrations on pages ix, 195 ©Asyam Design/stock.adobe.com

Illustrations on pages ii, x, 70, 250 ©Roni/stock.adobe.com

Illustrations on pages 32, 35, 49, 243 ©moleskostudio/stock.adobe.com

Illustrations on page 11, 77 ©OlgaKorneeva/stock.adobe.com

Illustrations on pages 96, 97, 255 ©Normform/stock.adobe.com

Illustrations on pages 145, 211 ©jakkapan/stock.adobe.com

Illustrations on pages 7, 150, 171, 184, 222 ©prasongtakham/stock.adobe.com

Illustrations on pages 24, 135, 234 ©smile3377/stock.adobe.com

Makeup by Codee Bradley

Hair styling by Paige Craft

FIRST EDITION

Designed by Nancy Singer

Library of Congress Cataloging-in-Publication Data has been applied for.

ISBN 978-0-35-867430-6

23 24 25 REP 10 9 8 7 6 5 4 3 2 1

CONTENTS

This is not a book about a talking dog. I know, I know, it's right there in the subtitle, but despite endless viral media headlines proclaiming it, dogs can't talk. At least not the way we do. Austrian philosopher Ludwig Wittgenstein once said, "If a lion could speak, we could not understand him," pointing to an experience of the world mostly unfathomable by human senses. Thankfully, Bunny is not a lion, and communication is greater than the sum of its parts. This is a story of a reckoning, both personal and cultural, human and nonhuman. This is what happens when curiosity and respect take precedence. When you give someone the opportunity to show you the nature of their world and can finally begin to reconcile your own. This is as much a story of me finding my voice as it is of Bunny exploring hers. Let's get into it, shall we?

I AM
BUNNY

1

Meeting Bunny

I watched Bunny's life begin through Facebook posts and was immediately drawn to her. She was about half the size of her siblings and had to fight a bit harder for food. And she had a perfectly round, little black dot on the top of her white head—like a bull's-eye for kisses.

Her breeder had named her Boston (the theme of the litter was state capitals), but I'd started thinking of her as Bunny almost immediately, even though I was number seven or eight on the wait list, so the likelihood that I'd get my pick wasn't high. Bunny was a word I used to refer affectionately to other people and animals in my life, but it felt like a proper name, not a nickname in this case.

She landed on this planet on July 28. A tiny 10.4-ounce, black-and-white tuxedo F1B sheepadoodle. (That means three quarters poodle and one quarter Old English Sheepdog.) She had ten littermates. That's a lot of puppies. How does one possibly choose? I suppose best practice is for the breeder to do the picking and make sure the puppy is matched with the right family, but this was a first-come, first-served situation. Her breeder recommended picking a first and second runner-up. I didn't have a second runner-up. Out of obligation to my heart, which may not have been able to cope with not getting my first and only choice (more so than out of obligation to the instructions given), I chose a second runner-up, another female pup, Helena. But I couldn't stop thinking about Boston. In fact, I remember next to nothing about Helena or why she made it into the top two. It was maddening not being there to get to know them—a unique combination of frustration, fear, and excitement, whose only outlet was extreme oversharing with family and friends.

Over that first month of watching their breeder post video updates about the litter of puppies on Facebook, I watched their personalities develop. I saw more of myself in Boston than in the others. She was curious and independent, always exploring the perimeters of the yard by herself. She was quiet and thoughtful, with what seemed like a touch of sarcasm. I remember watching her wiggle her way toward her mother's teat, only to be shoved out of the way by a larger pup, and I swear I saw her roll her eyes. "I *get* you," I thought to myself.

I'd found this breeder months before the puppies were due, chosen from a long list of other candidates within an eight-hour driving radius. I didn't realize I could fly with a puppy, but even if I had, somehow the idea of my future puppy being across the country or even just a few states away was painful. Like, as long as we were in the same state, I could shoot rays of love and connection and intention and some other woo-woo BS directly into my puppy-to-be.

My somewhat limited but still impactful prior experiences with dogs led me to believe that dedicating myself wholly to this new relationship was the next big adventure for me.

When the day came to meet her for the first time, she was one month old. For the first couple of weeks of life, puppies aren't really that interesting. I mean they're super-cool little developing beings, but their eyes and ears are closed, it's hard to get a sense of their individual personalities, and they just kinda eat and poop a lot. Their breeder recommended meeting them closer to eight weeks (so their personalities develop a bit and you get a better feel for who might be a good fit for your family), but I couldn't wait. I'm like this with everything. I chronically show up half an hour early to appointments. It's not even that I don't like to be late (which is true), I just get obsessed with doing the thing . . . perfectly . . . and immediately . . . and this was a really important thing. I was nervous. It was like a first date. I mean, I was pretty sure that she was the one for me, but what if she didn't like me? You can't force that. Would we have anything to talk about? Online dating is the ultimate comedy of errors. Lofty expectations wrapped up in a few cute pics, a carefully worded bio, and some brief, in-app small talk, followed by an awkward meet and greet and the immediate knowledge that you would like never to see this person again. This, of course, until one day it works, despite one's jaded incredulity. Is that what getting a dog is like? Clearly I was overthinking things, but that's what I do. Besides, a dog has to love you right? Even if you look nothing like your profile pic?

Online dating is how my husband, Johnny, and I met. I'd moved to Seattle from Kauai, created an OkCupid account, and gone on several dates that reminded me why I liked being single. I had changed my status after these dates from *looking for romance* to *looking for activity partners* (I figured maybe I could just make some friends, or at least attract a different type of person), so Johnny played it super cool when we were first talking, not coming on too strong. We talked for months, eventually taking it off the dating app and corresponding via email. It was nice to be able to get to know him this way, without pressure or expectation. Eventually I suggested we meet, and for our first date we climbed Red Mountain. He still played it cool as a cucumber. We stopped to get dinner after the hike, and he made me pay to ensure that I didn't think it was a "date" and also to ensure that there'd be a second, one that he could pay for. After dinner, he shook my hand. I laughed at him then and laugh now remembering that moment. It was the first time I hadn't just found myself in a relationship. This one was intentional on both of our parts, and we try to keep it that way now: evolving as healthy relationships do, while people grow, change, get new hobbies, get sick, go back to school, fall in and out of funks, change careers . . . taking care to maintain a deep foundational connection. At least that's the idea, right? Through thick and thin? I say all this because I believe that a relationship with a nonhuman requires a similar sort of open-ended expectation with a through line of love. That's what I had experienced with Johnny for the first time, and that's what I was ready to experience again with Bunny.

The breeder lived on the other side of the state, so the drive took five hours. I'd convinced my parents to road-trip out there with me since driving makes me anxious, Johnny had to work, and I was too excited to focus. I think they were tired of hearing me talk about nothing but impending "motherhood," and this trip had the potential to shut me up for a bit.

Haha . . . the joke was on them.

I spent most of those five hours looking at Facebook pics of tiny Boston (*Bunny!*), and I pretty much haven't talked about anything else since. I don't remember the days leading up to, or the days immediately following, our first "date," but that one day is fixed in the part of my brain that holds core memories.

Walking into the breeder's home, my stomach was in my throat. We went almost immediately into the whelping pen with Bunny, her siblings, and her mother, Domino. I sat down in the middle, and without hesitating, Domino came and lay down across my lap.

Surprised, the breeder said, "Wow, she never does that. She's usually pretty standoffish." I took it as a good sign. The puppies mostly ignored me. Some were sleeping, others were chewing on small toys. I resisted the urge to reach out and grab them, because I wanted to see what might happen naturally. After a few minutes, Bunny, who'd been crawling over some of her puppy siblings, looked directly into my eyes, beelined toward me, and crawled into the crook of my right arm, where she stayed for the full two hours I was there.

The breeder and I talked about the pups, and about life in general. We laughed about how many times a week I'd been calling (it was *many*). Toward the end of my time there, I wrapped my arm around Domino, silently thanked her for the gift she was giving me, and wept.

2

The Road to Bunny

It had taken me a couple of years to get Johnny on board with the idea of getting a dog . . . he's a cat guy.

I would ask, "What do you think about getting a dog?" Johnny would laugh uncomfortably, and I would break the tension by joining in the laughter, as if confirming I was only making a terrible joke.

This scene played out a couple of times a year, and I could tell he wasn't ready to even consider it. It wasn't just that he preferred cats either. Johnny and I were still going on rock-climbing and backpacking adventures all the time, road-tripping as often as we could. The commitment was too large, I knew it. And I was completely committed to the long-term success of our marriage, so we compromised and got a dog. Just kidding, not yet.

Cats are independent and easy—or at least his were. They'd come with the house when Johnny moved in on his own. A feral mother and daughter

who'd been coming around for food for the last few years. Johnny had grown up with dogs but found a love for feline companionship when these two, named Kiester and Spooky, finally started coming inside and claiming him as their human when he began leaving food out for them. They'd been sharing space for years before I finally joined the family, officially moving in a few years after we started dating.

Johnny and I decided long ago not to have children of our own (the human kind, anyway), but getting a dog felt akin to making the decision to have a child because of the high level of responsibility. I hadn't been ready to take on that kind of commitment before Bunny. I'd had to barrel through some pretty extreme obstacles to get to where the idea of raising a dog was sane adjacent.

But I felt ready now. Johnny and I owned our own home, and I was running a successful business from it. I was healthy, happy, and generally more stable than I'd ever been.

So, periodically, I would pose that question to Johnny. Then, sometime in mid-2019, Johnny went off script:

Me: "What do you think about getting a dog?"
Johnny: "Hm. Maybe a small one."

That was all the *yes* I needed. I started researching breeders that day. All I could think and talk about from that day forward was the dog we would soon welcome into our home. I didn't just regale my friends and family with the news, I brought it up with strangers. Several months after Johnny finally said yes, we officially became the human parents of a decidedly *not* small dog. Well, she was small for a minute.

Given my current lot in life (as Bunny the dog's mom), you might assume that I'd had many core memories involving dogs throughout my childhood. And by *core memory* I mean one that is of greater importance and recalled more vividly than an ordinary memory. I had plenty of experiences with dogs, even had a couple growing up, but until recently there was just one experience, one dog that I'd remembered again and again with both wonder and alarm.

I was young—four or five maybe?—and on a camping trip with my parents. We would regularly take our lime-green VW pop-top camper van into the desert or up to the mountains, which was the destination in this particular instance. Driving up to the mountains always freaked me out. The road seemed too narrow to be safe, especially with such a steep cliff looming over one side. I would spend most of the drive petrified we'd topple over the edge, so I'd persistently lean in the opposite direction as a safety precaution.

It was dark by the time we arrived, so my parents got right to work setting up camp. As they unloaded the car and pitched our tent, I wandered off to say hello to a couple at a nearby campsite. At some point while I was making friends with our new and temporary neighbors, I turned around and found myself face to face with the biggest dog I had ever seen in my life. It may as well have been Cerberus, the vicious three-headed watchdog of ancient Greek legend.

As the dog approached five-year-old me, I slowly walked backward, trying to keep distance between us. The dog continued to move toward me, causing my startled apprehension to give way to panic. I sped up, but I tripped over a rock and stumbled into a bonfire behind me. I'm not sure what happened next. Someone must have pulled me out of the fire, because only the palms of my hands sustained injuries.

This is my earliest memory of a dog. A hellhound—who, in retrospect, was probably quite sweet—and blistered palms. If you'd told me back then that I'd be writing a book about a dog someday, I never would have believed you. Life can be a real trip sometimes.

This experience didn't at all dampen my desire for animal companionship. I went to horse camp one summer, and upon my return relentlessly pestered my parents for a pony. I managed to wear them down enough that they eventually gave me an orange tabby kitten. I named him Napoleon, Polo for short, and he was a total buddy. Not long after his arrival, my parents adopted a red Doberman whom they named Darby. She loved my dad and carrots more than anything in the world. You'd think that my time with Darby might vividly outweigh the momentary experience I had with the "hellhound" when I was five, but memory is a strange thing, and that is not the case. When I met Darby for the first time at the shelter, I remember being somewhat nonplussed although I can't remember why. And I remember remembering the hellhound.

We had another dog after Darby passed. One whom, oddly enough, I can barely recall at all. His name was Bear, he was a Bouvier des Flandres. My mum says he was psychotic. That's about all I got. He was only with us for a short while, having run into the woods one afternoon and never returned. We speculated that he may have been shot or confused for an actual bear. Darby, who looked very much like a deer, had most certainly been shot by a BB gun at one point. She came home with a small wound that quickly ballooned as her chest filled with blood, and we raced her to the emergency vet. She was fine despite the fact that they weren't able to remove the pellet. She lived with it in her chest until old age eventually took her.

I was hoping I'd have the kinship my dad had with Darby with the dog Johnny and I decided to bring home, and now I can safely say that wish came true. I love Bunny so much that it's hard to remember a time before her, both in terms of our relationship and in terms of how that relationship has completely changed the trajectory of my life.

"Live in the moment" is a cliché that I've heard and fought for decades, despite living the majority of my life in exactly that way. Perhaps simply because I don't like being told what to do even if by a cliché not directed at me. It's too simple. No nuance. I'm skeptical of anything that pretends to be that easy.

When I was in kindergarten, I was sexually assaulted on the playground, and when I went to the attending teacher for help, she told me, "You brought this

on yourself." This wasn't the last time my body was used without my consent. It's obliteratingly sad how many women would be all too familiar with my stories, and this experience on the playground set in motion a framework of behavior and beliefs about myself that I've only recently come to reconcile and a need for the depth of connection with no strings attached that only a dog can offer.

The truth is, many of my past experiences were painful enough to avoid revisiting, and my future—although not bleak by any stretch of the imagination in 2019 (remember I said I was "stable")—was still governed by a seemingly random series of enterprises and undertakings guided mostly by luck or obsession. I was often impulsive, sometimes reckless, and consistently had no idea what I was doing, even when I was doing things well, which was a significant improvement over the prior decade.

Only recently have I come to a place where I'm usually comfortable examining, without judgment, the experiences that have made me who I am. I spend tremendous effort thinking about how my past has informed my personality in an effort to indeed become more mindful. The way I see it, my memories are creative re-creations, interpretations as opposed to absolute truths. But those interpretations inform my personality just as much as the objective facts of whatever happened in my past. My core memories, and the ways I choose to interpret them, become my core beliefs and values.

All of this is to say: As much as I hate the simplicity of "live in the moment," I can't deny that it's the foundation I've built my life on. It is, for better or for worse, a core value of mine. Because beneath all my anxiety and rough edges, I do believe that all I can do is make the best choice for myself in each moment—even when those choices are scary, even when they require me to take on big, Bunny-size life changes.

If someone out there has the secret to living a life you're proud of, DM me. Until then, I'll be here, stringing together my best efforts one moment at a time, hoping it leads to a life I'm proud to say I made for myself.

3

Bunny Meets Buttons

I spent several years imagining what life with a dog would look like. I'll tell you right now that it looks zero percent like what I'd expected it would. Maybe even less than zero percent.

People often ask me if I knew I was going to teach Bunny how to communicate by pressing recordable buttons when I got her. The answer is yes. Well, the answer is I knew I was going to try. I'd seen a dog "talking" with its owner online, and I was excited about the prospect that my dog might be able to talk to me too. I remember telling Johnny and friends that I was going to teach Bunny to use buttons to communicate; most of those people laughed uncomfortably in response but lauded my enthusiasm all the same. I wasn't hurt by their doubts, because I had my own. I thought it was possible that I might be successful, however improbable. I started by recording an OUTSIDE button and placing it by the door. Each button had a little speaker and microphone so you could record your own voice and play it back through the button. I pressed that button every time we went outside, paired with a hearty verbal dose of "outside" as well. I expected she'd need to hear a word a whole lot before it had any meaning to her. I could never have imagined the strange and wonderful journey we were about to embark upon, full of beautiful connected moments, astounding communication, and hard-learned, painful yet poignant lessons.

I devoured training books and blogs. I followed trainers on Instagram and YouTube and made our home puppy ready several months before Bunny came to live with us. I got a crate, food and treats, far too many toys, grooming supplies, and a doggy toothbrush. I got one of those pound-puppy-looking stuffed dogs that you put the hand warmer in, and there's a little battery-operated beating heart to make sure your pup is comfortable their first few nights in their new home. I got a leash and collar and harness and a special tag for her with her name on it.

And of course, I got buttons.

During my puppy research and prep, I'd found Christina Hunger, a speech-language pathologist in San Diego who had gone viral for teaching her dog, Stella, to communicate using recordable buttons. An article had come across my news feed directing me to her Instagram account. It talked a bit about her process and what she'd been able to accomplish with Stella.

I was eager to add this form of communication to an almost impossible list of relationship and communication goals I had for Bunny and me. I began reading about augmentative and alternative communication (AAC) and canine cognition in addition to training. Like I mentioned before, I didn't have any training experience, and I certainly didn't have any speech-language pathology experience. But what I did have was creativity, curiosity, and—according to some—an infuriatingly tenacious spirit.

I spent the first couple of weeks with Bunny focusing on building our bond, getting to know one another, and working on basic obedience. I'd never trained a dog before, or any animal for that matter, but through my research I felt I had a decent grasp on how to get started. A positive-reinforcement approach made the most sense to me. Positive reinforcement uses rewards to increase the likelihood that a behavior will be repeated. It's fun for both human and animal, and doesn't rely on punishment to accomplish training goals. It's also (obviously) way more nuanced than that, but those are the most basic basics. I got a clicker and stocked up on treats.

Throughout our day, we'd work on obedience training: sit, come, down, stay, focus, touch. Then we'd play, then nap, and then go for small walks. I made sure to incorporate specific visual cues for each verbal cue so that I'd be able to ask her to perform a task nonverbally as well. (This was mostly in case we were ever at the Oscars together, and I needed her to get me another bacon-wrapped asparagus and didn't want to interrupt the speaker, or vice versa.)

Here's an example of how I incorporated both visual and verbal cues: If we were walking down the street and someone stopped to chat, I could signal Bunny with a small hand gesture to sit or wait or come. As our verbal and nonverbal communication skills grew, I became more receptive and in tune with her intrinsic communications. It almost felt like I could read her mind. She would look at me when she was uneasy, as if to say, "What do we do?" I'd look back at her and silently say, "I got you, puppa. Don't worry about a thing."

We made quick progress with basic obedience. Bunny was eager to learn and seemed eager to please—or at least eager to sample whatever tasty snack was always in my hands. I couldn't get enough of it. Our bond and understanding of one another was deepening daily. I began to experiment with the buttons too. Every time we went for a walk, I would press OUTSIDE and say "outside" aloud to create a verbal association. Once we were outside I'd throw a little outside party, saying the word over and over again.

One day, when Bunny was around four months old, Johnny and I were sitting on the couch watching a movie while Bunny stood by her buttons looking

back and forth between the buttons and us. As we watched out of the corner of our eyes, she pressed OUTSIDE on her own, without any encouragement or modeling from us, for the very first time. "Did you just say outside?" I squealed. Her head whipped up proudly like she'd solved a riddle, ears flying outward. We ran—where else?—outside to celebrate.

It was game on after that. There was only one small problem: I didn't really have any idea of how to proceed. I found myself remembering this quote often attributed to Pablo Picasso: "Learn the rules like a pro, so you can break them like an artist." So, in an effort to learn the rules I was aiming to break, I began reading about AAC modeling best practices, about language development in children, and about canine cognition. It was all foreign to me. In some ways, my lack of scientific background in these areas may have protected me from inborn biases about what might be possible. I didn't have a clear scientific understanding of what had been tried before, whether successfully or unsuccessfully, so I was open to any outcome.

We affixed her OUTSIDE button to a plywood board with Velcro, and added three additional phrases: COME, PLAY, and LOVE YOU.

After some small successes with the buttons, I wanted to establish a training protocol in the same way that I had with our obedience training. My gut instinct was that using treats as motivation to interact with the buttons would muddy the word's intended meanings, so I decided from day one that I would never use food in conjunction with Bunny's language learning.

It took a while to get into a rhythm. I began speaking to Bunny all the time and emphasizing words that I imagined adding to the board in the future. Simple and straightforward concepts like "outside" and "play" were easy to model: I'd simply press the button, say the word out loud, then pair that with either going outside or playing. But I wanted Bunny to be able to express concepts that I wouldn't necessarily pick up on just by reading her body language. I wanted her to be able to tell me how she was feeling, and whether she was in pain, and who she wanted to play with and when. I wondered if it could be possible in some distant future for dogs to tell us about their dreams or their puppyhood traumas before adoption. My sense was that I could find moments wherein she or I were experiencing a certain emotional state and capture it by modeling the appropriate button and connecting a word to it.

For example, when she saw a bird on our deck, she'd stiffen and bark like the safety of her whole extended family depended on it. I interpreted that as "mad" and would model BUNNY MAD on the board, then say it several times as well. Or when Johnny would come home after a climbing trip, Bunny would become so excited she'd pee her pants. Then she'd wiggle and whimper and figure eight between his legs. Seemed like an appropriate time to model HAPPY. This process allowed us to add several buttons related to emotional states, although the question of how similar her emotions were to ours remained. I don't suppose we'll ever know exactly how someone or something else experiences a given emotion compared to our own experiences. At the same time my friend and I may have different perceptions of the color red—but we both still call it red.

Over time I've learned that many words can only be modeled effectively in conjunction with words she already knows well and uses regularly. Time-related buttons are a good example. While I'm still not certain that she fully grasps concepts like *yesterday*, *today*, and *tomorrow*, she seemed to pick up *now* and *later* rather quickly, as I was able to model them in conjunction with actions like "play." I'd press NOW PLAY and we would immediately begin to play. Then we would stop and I'd model ALL DONE PLAY. Similarly, if she requested PLAY, and I wanted to teach the concept of "later," I'd model PLAY LATER, set a fifteen-minute timer, and begin play as soon as it went off. Slowly we generalized that by extending the time. *Later* is a nebulous concept for me, and I suppose to her it simply means not now, but before I forget about it altogether.

I began incorporating daily button-training sessions into our routine. We would sit at the buttons and I would try to reinforce a new concept, repeating it and asking her questions in the hopes of garnering a contextually appropriate response. This struck me as the most logical way to increase her rate of learning. I'd say, "Let's play tug," then repeat with the buttons, and then we would play tug. While we were playing, I'd repeat "play tug, play tug" several times. After a few moments of that, we'd stop. I'd say, "All done play tug," then repeat with the buttons. We'd practice this several times, then I'd move on to holding the tug in front of her and asking "What?" and signaling toward the tug toy. She tended to become disengaged with *what* questions, which led me to realize that I needed a different approach.

What I found was that even without being reinforced with treats, the buttons were their own reward for Bunny. With this type of training, her primary reinforcer had become *being understood*. So if she didn't actively have something to express, she was less motivated to learn. I began spending much of my day near the buttons, whether I was working or relaxing, so that if an opportunity arose when Bunny felt compelled to explore her words, I'd be available to help. One day Bunny walked to the buttons and pressed NOW PLAY. I grabbed a ball, and a tug, walked over to the board, and asked her, "What play? Ball or tug?" and pointed to the part of the board that housed her toy buttons. She thought for a moment, then emphatically pressed TUG. These were both new buttons to her, so she hadn't cemented their position or association yet, but I acted quickly on her perhaps accidental press of TUG, thereby reinforcing her initial request, and reinforcing the hunch I'd had that Bunny setting the terms for this sort of learning would yield better results. Taking the opportunity to use even accidental button presses as teachable moments has proven invaluable.

Since then, I mostly let Bunny initiate conversation, and we work in language-learning moments when the opportunity arises naturally. For example, if she approaches the board and presses GO PARK and we've already been to the park, it's an excellent chance for me to model WENT PARK MORNING, thereby reinforcing a past tense and a time of day. Sometimes I'll ask questions that increase her motivation toward dialogue by saying something like, "When did we go park?" Many times it means that I model something with no expectation of response, like when we return from the park, I may model ALL DONE PARK, HOME NOW, SETTLE. But what it means in the grander scheme of things is that this remains fun for her, and that she always has the choice to opt in or out. I know from firsthand experience that being heard increases connection.

Bunny communicates perfectly without the buttons, as all dogs do (even if humans don't always understand those communications), but by giving her the agency to communicate in as many ways as possible, she remains curious, open, and full of potential.

Jane Goodall

Recently one of our followers on social media dubbed me "Jane Doodall." I've always had a deep reverence for Dr. Jane Goodall, who has dedicated her life to understanding chimpanzees and the conserving of their habitats. Even though dogs are a "human's best friend," and despite my sense that Bunny is my own actual human-not-human child, chimps are our closest living genetic relatives.

From an early age, Jane was obsessed with animals and even had a stuffed chimpanzee that went everywhere she did. As a young woman, she wanted to attend university, but couldn't afford it. But in 1957 she got an even better opportunity—traveling to Kenya to stay on a family friend's farm. There, she met Dr. Louis S. B. Leakey, who jump-started her scientific career. Dr. Leakey saw so much potential in Jane that he secured funding for her to study chimpanzees in the wild. She made her way by boat to the Gombe

Stream Game Reserve, where she methodically earned the chimps' trust and began her now world-famous work.

About this work Jane would later say, "I wanted to learn things that no one else knew, uncover secrets through patient observation. I wanted to come as close to talking to animals as I could."

Jane gave names to the chimps she began to encounter regularly, much to the chagrin of senior scientists, who believed that they should be numbered and not named. These scientists were resistant to the idea that chimpanzees could have personalities and emotions. (Insert eyeroll.) As Dr. Goodall said, "You can't share your life in a meaningful way with a dog, a cat, a rabbit, and so on, and not know the professors were wrong." Or, as one might say today, "Tell me you've never had a dog without telling me you've never had a dog."

David Greybeard was one of the chimps that first allowed Jane to observe him. An older and high-ranking male, his acceptance of Jane meant that others in the group also became more comfortable with her presence. On November 4, 1961, it was David who Jane first observed making and using a tool to collect termites. He'd pluck a thin branch from a tree, strip the leaves, and insert it into a termite mound, pulling it out covered in termites, which he'd then eat. Up until this point, creation and use of tools was thought to be a uniquely human trait. This was one of her most groundbreaking discoveries, and when she excitedly told Leakey her observations, he said, "Now we must redefine tool, redefine Man, or accept chimpanzees as humans."

(Cue me screaming in independent, empowered, tenacious female.)

She also discovered that chimps are omnivores, not herbivores as previously thought, and because of her work in Gombe (and without a graduate degree, I might add), she was accepted as a PhD candidate at Cambridge University in 1962. She earned her PhD in ethology (the study of animal behavior) in 1965 at the age of thirty-one. She continued her work in Gombe for the next twenty years, and with the help of *National Geographic*, who became a sponsor, she wrote and published her first book: *My Friends the Wild Chimpanzees*. It was aimed at the general public and enraged her scientific peers. (Hehehe!)

Since then, her achievements and contributions to science and conservation are far too numerous to name without turning this whole book into a Jane Goodall biography. But it's important to note that, in her late eighties, she continues her conservation work, traveling an average of three hundred days a year, speaking about climate change, threats to chimpanzee habitat, and other global crises.

Dr. Goodall is one of the preeminent badasses of our time. She announced that animals had feelings before it was popular to think so. Particularly inspiring to me, however, is her unyielding passion and belief in her own convictions in the face of so much criticism. She was once told that she couldn't follow her dreams because she was "just a girl." I relate to this. Nothing motivates me more than someone telling me I can't do something. It takes an extraordinary amount of courage to blaze one's own path through uncharted territory against all odds, but that's what she's done and continues to do. Not only is Dr. Goodall showing the world that we can learn more about humans by observing primates, but also how we can become better humans by appreciating their complexities. And she does it with grace and intelligence, creating her own road map every step of the way.

4

Learning Her "Language"

Dogs have the most amazing system of communication, and learning about canine body language has been one of my favorite parts of getting to know Bunny. Dogs are at their most obvious when they are growling, barking, snapping, and biting—signs that there is cause for alarm, at least in your dog's mind. But before they get to those highly visible, robust cues, dogs tell us a lot with other actions of body language that are actually quite obvious and informative once you know what to look for. (And I'd be lying if I said I didn't personally relate to a lot of them.)

These subtle actions are called canine *displacement behaviors*. Your dog may exhibit these behaviors when they are experiencing anxiety or uncertainty and are trying to de-escalate a situation. Engaging in an actual fight isn't economical for dogs, so they are masters of conflict avoidance. Even the loud and scary growls, barks, lunges, and snaps are often ritualized aggression meant to send a message, but not start a fight. Evolutionarily speaking, there is too much to lose.

You'd think perhaps that after twenty to forty thousand years of coevolution, we'd be champs at reading our nonhuman besties. From competitors as apex predators to partners in domestication, the wolves that became dogs, newer theories suggest, started as waste removers for hunter-gatherer humans—eating scraps of food, of course, but also human feces. These wolves, who were naturally more tolerant and less fearful of humans, thrived on the caloric surplus and thus self-selected generation after generation, as these traits would have been evolutionarily advantageous. Slowly they evolved into an early iteration of our modern-day dog. Dogs are not only the oldest domesticated animal, but the only one who became domesticated during humans' hunter-gatherer period. All others were domesticated when farming became widespread, and humans became more stationary. In Israel, the remains of an elderly man and a puppy buried together are dated back to around fourteen thousand years ago. In burial, the man's hand was placed on the puppy, showing the importance of this partnership even then. Despite our lengthy partnership, it seems we are born woefully unprepared for nonverbal communication with another species.

Common canine behaviors include yawning, sneezing, lip licking, full-body shaking, marking, and ground sniffing. But the trick to recognizing when they become canine displacement behaviors is to watch for actions that are happening out of context. For example, if it's close to bedtime or after some physical activity and your dog yawns, they're likely tired. But if your dog isn't tired, and you set the nail clippers down beside them intending to trim their nails, they may sniff them then yawn in displacement because the sight of the clippers makes them nervous. If you're walking your dog and they periodically pause to sniff the grass, a tree, or a fire hydrant, it's probably just information gathering. But if your dog sees another dog approaching and starts immediately sniffing the ground, it may be displacement because they're feeling conflicted or uncertain.

Dogs also use calming signals that can look a lot like displacement behaviors. They are used to diffuse tension and avoid conflict when they feel threatened. When meeting a new dog, if Bunny is uncomfortable with the greeting (which she almost always is), she will avert her gaze, flick her tongue, and possibly yawn or pant. If the other dog reads these signals and backs off, she'll do a full-body shake and return to floppy, happy Bunny. If these signals are not respected, she may escalate by growling or snapping, all completely appropriate and natural forms of communication in dogs. During play, you might see sneezing as a calming signal, which is the dog's way of continuing to be nonthreatening. Calming signals function directly in social interactions, and displacement behaviors are more of a release or discharge of discomfort.

My job, as Bunny's guardian, is to notice these subtle signs, which help me to analyze her triggers, remove her from these situations, and potentially countercondition her so they aren't as alarming to her in the future. I can set up scenarios in which the meeting is more controlled, at a greater distance, or just not at all. These signs are valuable information about her state of mind.

I have my own challenges with direct communication. I'm a people pleaser while also being a people avoider. Historically, I've not known how to properly advocate for myself, which has gotten me into some pretty sticky situations—especially when the other person doesn't pick up on my nonverbal signals. I find it difficult at times to be assertive. In my own mind I'm constantly communicating nonverbally, just like Bunny. I might shift my body to signal moving away from the conversation, look around at the environment to cue a lack of engagement, give my attention to my phone, or take a sudden and intense interest in my cuticles. Muscle tension in my body and my face expresses discomfort, as does a grimace instead of a smile. There are so many.

Even verbally, I use all the classic phrases to signal that I'm disinterested. Don't tell me you're not familiar with these—who hasn't resorted to repeating "Oh wow, that's crazy" when stuck in a conversation you don't want to be in? Repeating that phrase alone should be a clear indicator of disengagement. But that's the thing: humans generally aren't very good at hearing and seeing nuance. It's not entirely our fault, though. We're all coming to the metaphorical table with unique backgrounds, cultures, and intersectional identities. It's a lot to keep track of, assuming you're aware enough even to know what the other person's nonverbal cues would look like.

Some of us are more adept at tuning in to the cues people give off. I myself am hyperaware of the unspoken, which is run-of-the-mill hypervigilance stemming from trauma. I know some of y'all feel me on that one. If we were all able to really pay attention to what a person might be saying before they have to say anything at all, so many interactions would go much more smoothly. The body rarely lies, and sometimes the body is the only part of us that can communicate the truth of how we're feeling or what we're thinking. Would it be easier if we could always communicate these sensations with words? Of course. But spelling things out can be far too intimidating, threatening, or overwhelming for some of us.

But, as the old saying goes: practice makes perfect. So let's practice picking up on common human nuances by using some of our shared displacement behaviors and calming signals within an imagined human context. It'll be fun. At the very least, it might convince you that these behaviors are actually more clear and direct than most humans think.

HYPOTHETICAL 1:

I am waiting in line to pick up an order from my favorite local Thai restaurant (fresh rolls are my go-to). I'm watching funny panda videos on my phone. I especially love the one where the baby sneezes and scares the crap out of its mom (so cute). The person behind me taps my shoulder. I turn around. They say, "How 'bout those Seahawks, huh?" "Um," I say, "I don't know much about sportsball, sorry," and go back to my phone. They continue with, "But you saw that touchdown, right?" Not knowing how to proceed, I yawn exaggeratedly and avert my gaze. "It was a total Hail Mary." First yawn obviously didn't work. Let's try again. I summon my inner dog lion and yawn with the breadth of a roar. At this point he would say something like, "Oh, I see you're busy, sorry for interrupting."

Efficacy rating: 7/10. It should not require two yawns.

HYPOTHETICAL 2:

Bunny and I are walking down a residential street. I'm listening to a podcast, Buns is happily sniffing all the smells, we are in the zone, doing our thing. A stranger approaches and signals for me to remove my headphones. I do so begrudgingly, and they say, "Hey! What kind of dog is that? Can I pet it?" and before waiting for a response they move quickly toward Bunny's face. We sidestep their advance, and I grumble under my breath, "We need space." The stranger looks confused and slightly offended, but continues walking.

Efficacy rating: 8/10. It was a close call.

My personal favorite of all the displacement behaviors is the full-body shake-off. I know from personal experience that this one works. So I'm going to ask you to do something with me. Stand up for a moment and bring to mind a particularly stressful event or emotionally charged interaction (don't worry, it'll only be with you for a few moments). Let yourself feel the frustration, anxiety, disappointment, regret. Stand with it, until it is almost too much to bear, then slowly start shaking your head. Then faster. Let the momentum build and move down through your body like a hurricane. Imagine, as the energy builds, that water droplets of shitstorm are being flung from your body with the ferocity of a nuclear reaction. Shake until you feel liberated and repeat as necessary.

Efficacy rating: 10/10. Dogs are so fucking smart.

I ignored my own subtle nonverbal cues for so long it created dysfunction, but this practice of tuning in to Bunny's has helped me to tune in to my own and begin to honor and meet my needs in a new way. When there are no words, you're forced to pay a lot more attention to the silences. It's a gift and a challenge that I heartily accept.

5

Expectation
vs. Reality

I adore Bunny to the depth of my core, but she also drives me crazy. All relationships require patience and compromise, and ours is no exception.

Bunny can be quite affectionate, but she isn't what I would describe as snuggly, and her sweetness is always given out on her own terms. As it should be, I suppose. I guess I'd had this idea that dogs just sort of want cuddles all the time? I know. It's an objectively silly thought. I don't want cuddles all the time and would lose my ever-loving mind if someone demanded them of me. Just the thought makes me mad. Not to mention that if you're getting a dog just so that you have something fluffy to hold when you're feeling out of sorts, might I instead recommend a weighted blanket, a heating pad, or one of those giant teddy bears that they have at raves and Burning Man? So although I may have hoped for a cuddlier fluff noodle, when she does occasionally put herself in my personal space for a prolonged period of time, I know that she's doing it because she genuinely

wants to. And in those moments, I feel like I have been supernaturally blessed. Big opinions mean bigger payoffs when we're eventually on the same page.

This need to be independent means that Bunny has strong feelings about everything, but especially her personal space. These feelings can create conflict at times. For example, she likes sleeping on the bed with us, but if there is a cat already there? That will not be tolerated in the slightest. Bunny's go-to method is to throw a tantrum until she is the last animal standing. We're working on that.

In some cases, Bunny's opinions are literally impossible to cater to. After all that effort to get the cat off the bed so she can hop up, she'll only enjoy being on the bed if we remain absolutely still. If we move at all, like even just a toe, she'll snarl with offense and take her business elsewhere.

The thing about giving your dog buttons to press is that they will quite literally be able to press buttons when they want to annoy you. If I'm working or in a meeting and unable to respond to her use of the buttons, she'll begin spamming the POOP or POTTY buttons as though I haven't taken her out in days. And then when I do let her out, she immediately comes back in, having done no business, only to continue spamming in a more urgent and messier fashion than before, using her back paws to express utter disgust until I break, no longer capable of working. Sometimes I'll realize that I needed a break, too, and I'll give my attention to Buns for a bit. Sometimes I just need to find a cardboard box for her to destroy. That usually works. Most of the time, she just needs me to be somewhere in the room making intense eye contact with her. Or, at the very least, watching her while she stares off into space, mentally exploring the space-time continuum.

But even this snarky behavior can have its charming moments. These days her go-to during meetings is to say BYE or STRANGER ALL DONE, both of which I find pretty funny. I don't know any humans who haven't wanted to say one of these things at some point during a meeting that could have been an email. I love this unapologetic quality in Bunny; she says what she thinks and doesn't care if other people like it. The other day, after a cameraman hovered for just a little too long over Bunny's buttons, Bunny got between him and the board and emphatically pressed SETTLE.

The first major personality difference I noticed between Bunny and me is that Bunny is loud. Like very loud. I missed this fact in my research, but poodles are amazing—and very, very loud—watchdogs. At least mine is. And Old English Sheepdogs as a herding breed like to be in control. Not all of them, of course, but these characteristics are a perfect storm in Buns. I used to go through my days unaware of the various birds landing on our deck. I paid no attention to the leaves blowing past our windows, our neighbors whispering two doors down, or the almost imperceptible sound of our house settling. I now notice all these things all the time, because Bunny's top priority is to alert me to these things by screaming about them at roughly 180 decibels.

And it's always a surprise. On more than one occasion, I have been violently jolted out of a quiet moment of work, quite literally throwing coffee in my own face, because Bunny has decided that the bee minding its own business just outside the window was a national security threat. Nailed it, Bunny.

Whether it's a partner, a child, a roommate, or a pet, many of us have to figure out how to successfully cohabitate with another being at some point in our lives. This doesn't become less true just because you're cohabitating with a dog instead of another human. And yelling "Unsubscribe" at your barking dog is ineffective. I know, because I've tried. Most actions that work to resolve challenges with other humans are ineffective with dogs. But one thing I've learned with Bunny is that this doesn't mean it's impossible, or even harder, to find solutions. It just requires a different strategy—one that works for both of us.

Johnny and I employ several strategies to navigate her ferocious, watchdog poodle voice: 1) we gently try to mitigate these events through counterconditioning; 2) we put up curtains; and 3) I now avoid overly full beverage cups. Because sometimes shit happens.

We're all people, even if we're dogs.

I'm No Scientist

I've said before and I'll say it again. . . . I do not believe that there has ever been an example anywhere of a nonhuman expressing an opinion, or asking a question. Not ever. It would be wonderful if animals communicated propositionally—i.e., could say things about the world, as opposed to just signaling a direct emotional state or need. But they just don't.

—*Geoffrey Pullum, linguist at the University of California, Santa Cruz*

With all due respect to Mr. Pullum, Bunny has some pretty big opinions she expresses quite clearly, even without buttons. It's clear that Bunny thinks Beacher and Selena, our neighbor's dogs, are a better hang than most dogs around here. You can feel her joyful exuberance at seeing them. The gentle swish of her tail, loose body language, relaxed face, pretend sneezes showing that she's not a threat. You can tell she's extra joyful when she purses her lips, stomps her feet, and lets out a "rooroo." She only does that for people or dogs she really loves. Bunny also has a variety of opinions about crows. Namely, that she does not want them on our deck, and the best way to handle trespassing crows starts by seething. Her high-flagging tail, tense face, and generally stiff body posture give it away long before she yells at and charges them. And I'd go so far as to suggest that she is constantly asking me questions without buttons. As a particularly sensitive dog, Bunny frequently looks to me to gauge the level of a perceived threat. If a person approaches from the other end of the beach, and Bunny doesn't recognize them, but I can see that they're one of her friends, she'll stiffen, then look to me for information. I'll say, "That's your friend Shannon!" And Bunny will immediately soften, stomp, and roo. In the aforementioned instance she is certainly signaling an emotional state, which I can read without her looking at me, and the need she has is for information. That's what a question is: a sentence worded or expressed so as to elicit information.

It's the context of any given interaction that gives Bunny's button presses validity. She begins her interactions by approaching the board, then waiting for eye contact, starting off with very clear communicative intent. Then she presses a button or combination of buttons and makes eye contact again, awaiting a response. Then I respond, then she responds. We take turns trying to understand and be understood. She'll use her body to offer more information, by looking at something specific, walking to the door, grabbing a specific toy after pressing PLAY, wagging her tail when I get it, or dropping her tail when I don't.

And it's not just me with whom Bunny communicates in this way. Her list of close human friends is quite small, but at the top of it, right up there with mom and dad, is Shannon. She's one of those humans who exude calm-strong energy, like she's seen some shit and she's going to make sure that you don't have to. Bunny's entire body lights up when I say "Shannon." If Bunny's paw accidentally activates the SHANNON button, she'll whip around and stare at me like, "No way! Why didn't you tell me Shannon was coming over?" When she realizes what she's done, she'll grumble her way softly to her bed for a good pout. If Johnny and I want to go out of town but can't take Bunny,

Shannon stays with her at our place, and I am delightfully bombarded with videos and pics of the two of them cuddling their days away (to an extent that I'm not too proud to admit makes me a tad jealous). But Bunny is still Bunny and makes her opinions about personal space known. Shannon is great at engaging Bunny with the buttons. She'll ask and model questions, and wait patiently when Bunny approaches the board. On one particular occasion, Bunny was standing at the board looking expectantly at Shannon, who walked to the buttons and modeled WHAT BUNNY WANT DO? Bunny stood in thought. After a long pause Shannon reached toward Bunny's ear to offer some scritches. Buns deftly dodged her hand and promptly pressed PLEASE NO THANK YOU, then walked away. Slay, opinionated and polite queen.

We gave Bunny pronouns. I, you, and we. Now those are some statistical improbabilities if I've ever seen any. I spent a few days modeling them contextually, and then one evening we decided to order takeout and Johnny left to go pick it up. Moments after he left, Bunny walked over to the board and pressed WE LOVE YOU WHY WENT.

"Why Dad went?" I asked. "Dad went to get food, we love Dad. Dad home soon," I continued. Bunny paused for a moment, then pressed DAD BYE. "Dad bye, that's right," I said. "Dad home soon."

So what we seem to have here is a plural pronoun used to express a group emotion, followed by a question and then a past-tense verb, followed by an observation, all of which was contextually appropriate to the situation. Or we have a dog stepping on random buttons. But from my seat on the couch, it looked a lot like probability.

People often ask me how I found out about the buttons and why I decided to use them with Bunny. The "how" is pretty straightforward: I saw a dog using them online, and after a bit of research, I found another dog, Sofia, taught by Alexandre Rossi in the early 1990s (I talk a bit more about him later on). It seemed like the buttons could be a way for me to achieve a deeper level of connection with my dog. Who wouldn't want that?

I want to make sure I'm clear about one thing, though: there's a big difference between wanting to see if my dog would enjoy this tool enough to continue to use it of her own volition and forcing her to interact with the buttons because I needed her to embrace them. Yes, I wanted to use as many resources to connect with Bunny as possible, but the buttons were only one of the tools I used to create this deeper bond. Frankly, the buttons wouldn't have been useful in creating that bond had I neglected to create a foundation of trust in other, more traditional ways. Exercising with her, playing with her, giving her skill training with positive reinforcement, giving belly scritches, meeting her needs consistently, and ensuring she feels safe in her environment—these things, and more, as mapped out in Maslow's hierarchy of needs, aren't as flashy as buttons, but they were more vital to creating the bond I wanted with Bunny. If connecting with my dog was a video game, the buttons are more like a bonus level that Bunny and I unlocked after completing the rest of the levels.

If Bunny had hated the buttons, I would never have forced her to use them.

This is something internet trolls call into question constantly. Look, I understand why some people are suspicious about my intentions. I know that it's bold to claim that I didn't care whether my dog would use the buttons, given that Bunny has become something of the poster dog for them. At the end of the day, I'll never be able to prove to naysayers that Bunny's success wasn't some diabolical scheme I'd come up with to get internet followers. All I can really offer in response is that forcing Bunny to use the buttons, or secretly using tricks off-camera to capture specific button presses, or whatever else people think I'm doing, are all antithetical to my goal. I want to connect with my dog and do what's best for her because I love her. Period.

Bunny took to the buttons quickly. Watching her interact with them, it seemed pretty undeniable to me that something cool was happening, but I didn't know if this was actually what it looked like: that my dog was communicating with words by pushing buttons. So when the opportunity presented itself to test things out with a legit team of scientists, I took it.

Around seven months after bringing Bunny home, and twenty-four buttons into our canine AAC journey, I came across a post on Facebook by Leo Trottier, a cognitive scientist in San Diego. He had founded a company called FluentPet and he was looking for beta testers for a canine-specific AAC device that he was developing. My interest was piqued and I was excited about the potential of having scientists help inform some of the decisions I made. We scheduled a phone call that set in motion a series of events that have inexorably shifted the way I look at communication. Given that Bunny was having so much success with these buttons already, I jumped at the opportunity to work with Leo. I wanted to get more insight into Bunny's experience. How could Bunny process language from a cognitive-science perspective? Were the buttons actually helping us communicate?

As it so happens, a personal visit to our home from Leo for the filming of a televised "Dog of the Year" piece was one of the first indications to me that

Buns had significantly bigger feelings than I knew. The film crew wanted to get a shot of Leo and me looking at the issue of the *Wall Street Journal* we were in (our first major publication). Leo came to join me on the couch, and as he sat Bunny screamed and lunged at his face. It was terrifying but two things became clear: that Bunny had incredible bite inhibition (she had very clearly made her point to Leo by drawing a single drop of blood in the center of his forehead); and that I had some work to do in terms of thoroughly understanding canine behavior. And hers specifically.

Something I'd gotten used to on social media was trolls claiming that what I was doing with Bunny was not science. In the beginning, this was true since there were no rigorous and systematic studies to prove that results could be reproduced or that this wasn't a series of coincidences. The trolls were correct when they said that mine was a sample size of one.

That changed once I started collaborating with Leo. Leo was working with Federico Rossano, the director of the Comparative Cognition Lab at UCSD. Together, they were planning a research study to analyze the utterances of the thousands of dogs and cats now pursuing button communication. Basically, Bunny had found her scientific community.

To be clear, I've always identified as an artist, not a scientist. That hasn't changed now that I'm working with scientists and research facilities. I don't have the schooling, degrees, or qualifications to call myself a scientist, and I would never pretend otherwise. That said, this realm of academia and science has been an interesting one to find myself in, and the more I get to know it, the more similarities I discover between how my brain works and how the scientists' brains seem to work.

At their core, art and science are rooted in a similar place. Curiosity guided by a deep longing to understand both ourselves and our environment in a more profound way, and to reveal the unknown. Artists and scientists alike can agree that the image of a dog asking its human for help with an earache is compelling.

I witnessed this exact thing last summer when Bunny pressed OUCH OUCH EAR HELP after shaking her head, then walked over to me and laid her head sideways in my hand. I flushed her ears, per my vet's recommendations, and all was well.

I'm engaged with the scientific community because I'm curious and because it offers perspectives I don't have. I want to know everything I can about the things that matter to me, even if the answers are not what I'd expect. Exploration of novel or controversial ideas by a community of like-minded individuals can influence social paradigms, and there are a few pet paradigms that I believe need some influence. It's time for science to catch up to what many of us already know—that our animal companions have a lot to say.

Gua, Viki, and Washoe

The most famous talking animal has to be Koko the gorilla. (And if you don't know Koko, stay tuned, she's discussed later in the book.) But I want to tell you about a few notable primates that paved the way long before Koko came onto the scene. Their names are Gua, Viki, and Washoe.

In the 1930s, comparative psychologists Winthrop Niles Kellogg (I swear to God, old-timey names are the absolute best) and his wife, Luella, decided to raise a toddler chimpanzee. As you do. They named the chimp Gua and raised her alongside their human son, Donald, who was a toddler when Gua joined the family. The Kelloggs wanted to see if a chimpanzee raised as a human would therefore learn to act like one, think like one, and even communicate like one.

For nine months, Winthrop and Luella conducted tireless experiments with both Gua and Donald. In what might be the best plot twist ever, the Kelloggs abruptly ended the tests because Donald started moving about on all fours, vocalizing to demand food the way Gua would, and had become increasingly aggressive, biting and scratching others.

In short: they discovered that it was Donald who was learning from Gua, not the other way around. Fascinating, right?

Viki was a chimpanzee adopted by Katherine and Keith Hayes in the late 1940s. They raised Viki as a human baby and physically manipulated her mouth to help her produce humanlike utterances. She passed away after only seven years and was only ever able to roughly say *mama*, *papa*, *cup*, and *up*. With what we know today this all just seems so, so reckless and unethical (and, like, totally illegal, right?).

And then there's Washoe, the first primate to use ASL (American Sign Language)—named after Washoe County, Nevada, where she was raised. In the 1960s, psychologists Beatrix and Allen Gardner had come to recognize that spoken language with chimpanzees wasn't possible due to anatomical differences between us and them. But observing that they frequently used gestures to communicate, the Gardners posited that ASL might be a much simpler and more productive way to explore language with a chimp. Turns out it was. She, too, was raised as though she were a human child, but by age five she had learned around three hundred fifty words and sparked the imagination of many professionals in the field.

Washoe lived in her own trailer in the Gardners' backyard, complete with homey amenities such as a kitchen, a bathroom, and a bedroom. There was even an intercom video system so they could monitor her. She did have house rules, though. One was that she wasn't allowed to get into the refrigerator at night. Robert Sapolsky, a Stanford neuroendocrinologist and primatologist, visited Washoe and recounts during a lecture how they caught her on camera sneaking to the fridge signing *Quiet Washoe, quiet Washoe.*

Duane Rumbaugh, scientist emeritus of the Great Ape Trust of Iowa, called it "absolutely frontier-breaking work." It is said that Washoe was able to combine words to express novel concepts. Upon seeing a swan, she once signed *water* and *bird.* (Critics, however, say that she was simply labeling the two things she saw—water and a bird.) She was also said to be self-aware, and when asked what she saw when looking in a mirror, she signed *Me, Washoe.* Plenty of questions were left unanswered by this incredible chimpanzee, but she definitely ushered animal language research into its wild heyday in the 1970s.

7

Yeah No
Nope No Thanks

had agreed to help produce a small New Year's Eve segment for TikTok, and in classic "me" style, I hadn't succeeded in directly saying no to their scripted request, despite my best intentions. I set the scene by covering Bunny's board in empty champagne bottles, tacky New Year's Eve decorations, all her toys, and a few socks. Utter *tohubohu*, my very favorite word, which means "chaos, disorder, and confusion."

Bunny took one look at the mess and pressed OOPS THIS PLEASE NO OOPS, then walked away.

Imagine saying exactly what you mean, every single time, without second-guessing how it will be received, because you simply don't know how to be inauthentic. No culturally selective pressures have ever told you that it isn't okay to just be yourself. IMAGINE!

This is one of the most important lessons Bunny is teaching me: the power of authenticity. Bunny is completely and unapologetically exactly who she is, which is decisive and self-possessed almost all the time. I have no idea where she gets this from, but it's certainly not her human mother. I wish I could be as assertive as Bunny is. She makes *no* look so easy.

I could've saved myself a ton of trouble and spent way less money on therapy if I'd learned how to say *no* earlier in life. Like, did I want to cover the majority of Gwen's shifts because she was too hung over and I was the lone coworker whose number she'd saved in her phone? No. Did I do it anyway? Yes. Yes, I did.

This drastic difference between Bunny's personality and my own has never been clearer than it was recently, when we had a film crew in our home. There were strangers, large equipment, and some inordinately unreasonable expectations placed on a puppy. The producer handed me a piece of paper. I skimmed through the words on the page and realized that this would be one of those moments where *no* would really come in handy.

"Is . . . is this a script for Bunny? You know, it doesn't really work that way," I said.

"Well, let's just try it," he replied.

So I said *yes*, like I do. The producer thought I was saying *Yes, I'll try*. In reality, I'd actually just agreed to scream internally while *they* tried, because I knew their idea would never work, but I am more comfortable saying *yes* than saying *no*.

Bunny, on the other hand, showed me how it's done. She made it clear—in no uncertain terms—that she was not into their script, nor would she pretend to care about it to make things easier for them. Instead, she said *no* in her own way. She licked my face, growled at the cameraman, and headed to the couch to supervise from afar.

This was the first of many such media encounters in our home. It quickly became clear that I'd have to learn how to say no—not just for me, but for

Bunny. It's my job to notice what's going on with Bunny and make sure she feels safe and comfortable. I'm the adult, the human, her parent, her liaison, her guardian. Bun knows how to say no, but she should not feel like she *has to.* Which is how interviews about Bunny quickly turned into lessons for me on how to say no.

I got to put the practice into action a few months later, when there was another film crew in our home. The situation was similar—strangers and large equipment—but this time there were fewer unreasonable expectations placed on a puppy because, well, I'd been making progress with my nos. We were nearing the end of the interview, which is when Bunny is usually expected to "perform." I was tired, she was tired, but I wanted the crew to get the shots they needed. I could feel my anxiety rising. Then, as if on cue, Bunny walked to the buttons and pressed SOUND BYE GO STRANGER, taking it upon herself to say what we'd both been thinking.

"I think we're done here," I said, backing her up.

8

You Look Flushed

Ever unleashed a fart bomb so offensive that your dog left the area? Sure, yeah, me neither. But if you have, you know firsthand that dogs are aware of our bodily functions. Dogs are known for their incredible sense of smell. As well they should be, because it's true: they have up to 300 million olfactory receptors in their boopable little snoots. Humans, by comparison, have a measly 5 million. Imagine the smells we miss out on. It's more than just a good sense of smell, though. Scientists speculate that a dog's self-awareness may stem primarily from their olfactory sense.

Traditional self-awareness tests have been performed with mirrors. A scientist will mark an animal's forehead with a dot of paint or something equivalent, then give them access to a mirror to see if they then try to touch or remove the mark on themselves. If they do, the theory goes that they recognize that they're looking at themselves in a mirror and therefore have self-awareness.

Several animals have succeeded at this test, including dolphins, elephants, great apes, and even magpies—but not dogs. And it's arguably an unfair method of testing self-awareness in dogs anyway, given that their superpower is smell. So alternate tests have been devised wherein dogs are provided with samples of their own urine (a sort of olfactory mirror) and another dog's urine. They consistently spend significantly less time sniffing their own piss than that of a stranger, which seemingly indicates that they might be thinking, *Yeah yeah yeah, that's my own piddle . . . boring.*

Science also tells us that smell is one of the senses most closely tied to memory. The smell of bleach, for example, transports me back to my childhood swim team and resurrects a memory wherein I challenged myself to swim the entire length of the pool underwater, pretending I was a mermaid. When I smell hay or manure, a scent many find off-putting, I remember the aroma of the rhinoceros exhibit as I walked into the San Diego Zoo with my grandfather. Of course, like every other type of memory, not all olfactory memories are warm and fuzzy. Any time I smell the sickly sweet and phony stench of fake bananas, I relive the first time I blacked out from drinking as a teenager, and I am instantly nauseated. (Why do teenagers think vodka infused with artificial fruit flavor is a great idea?)

Dogs' memories too are strongly linked to scent. They have the ability to remember dog friends by smell even after having spent years apart. They can assess another dog's emotional state, tell where they've been, what they've eaten, who they've been playing with, and so much more that we just have no idea about, with just a quick sniff. Def a superpower.

As much sense (heh) as all this makes, I could not have anticipated that Bunny would use her smell superpower to unabashedly call Johnny out after he'd taken care of some business.

It was a cool spring day. I was working in the living room, responding to some emails. Johnny came out of the bathroom, poured himself another cup

of coffee, then left the room to head upstairs. Bunny looked at me, then at the stairs, then again at me, pranced over to the board, and pressed DAD POOP.

Now, I am a dedicated teacher when it comes to showing Bunny how to properly communicate with buttons. I want to help her develop an organized syntactic structure, which means I have a responsibility to model things back to her with the board, even when I'm trying not to die laughing. So that's exactly what I did. I tried my best to compose myself, walked over to the board, and modeled DAD WENT POOP with buttons.

"Dad WENT poop," I said, before I dissolved into giggles of childlike delight.

This is a good time for a brief primer on how I capture the videos I post on social media. I typically start filming as soon as Bunny approaches the board. Then, if she decides to use the buttons, I edit out the long periods where both of us are standing around in silence and post the actual button presses.

On this particular day, Bunny had been standing at her buttons and observing us for a few minutes, so I had been recording and managed to cap-

ture the moment on my iPhone. I edited the video, as I usually do, and posted it while still giggling. I did wonder if I should maybe ask Johnny if he'd be all right with me posting a video of our dog calling him out for pooping. But in the end, I decided that not sharing this would be a crime against science and comedy, so I posted it.

The day after I posted the video, I got a DM from the post-poop bathroom spray brand Poo-Pourri asking if they could share the video across their channels. Shortly thereafter our DAD POOP video went viral, and I had no other choice but to come clean to Johnny about his unexpected turn as a social media darling. Lucky for me, he was a great sport about the whole thing.

About a month later, the poop hype died down a bit and Bunny and I started working on tenses and dialogue with her buttons. Then, one day Bunny walked to the board and pressed WHERE DAD. I responded by pressing the buttons and repeating with words, "Dad upstairs."

Bunny paused for a moment, the way she does when she's considering her next words, then decisively pressed DAD POOP WENT.

The part of me that's committed to the scientific process would have rewarded her for an elegant and accurate utterance. Unfortunately, the human in me was too busy laughing and muttering "Ohhhh noooooo . . ." I'm not going to lie to you, all of this was hysterical. Watching Bunny give Johnny crap for crapping was very fun for me.

What was less fun, though, was when Bunny asked me one day, out of nowhere, MOM POOP WHERE.

It took a minute for me to register that she wasn't asking where she was going to go poop, but rather where Mom poops. Ever dedicated to the process, I answered Bunny's question by taking her on a field trip to our bathroom and showing her the toilet, hoping that would be enough clarification. Much to my dismay, it did not stop Bunny from finding this topic of conversation endlessly fascinating. A few days later, she finally called me out by pressing YOU WENT POOP. I was so impressed with her perfect syntax, I almost forgot to be embarrassed.

The questions raised by this interaction really make me wonder how our dogs might experience the world differently from us. How much of a sense of our sameness and our difference do they have? Does it bother her that there are dissimilar standards for us? Why do we pee and poop inside, and then make it disappear? I wonder what dogs think as we hastily rush them past the fire hydrant that tells a million tales or prevent them from sniffing Aunt Betsy's butt because it's "rude." These must be the most baffling moments to them. What does poop smell like when you have 300 million olfactory receptors? A lot of dogs seem to think it smells good enough to eat. The depth of a dog's use of olfactory cues in communication and our ignorance of that fact can only serve to confound them. At any rate, this is why I generally let Bunny walk me. I love watching her explore the world in a way I never can.

That's the beauty of doing this work with Bunny: I don't settle for assuming I know why she does or does not enjoy things. I can try to give her the vocabulary to express things I wouldn't have considered. I believe that open lines of communication begin with empathy. When you attempt to see the world through someone or something else's eyes, you welcome experiences that didn't exist before. The compassion that comes with this can only lead to deeper understanding and connection, and is that not ultimately what we are all here for?

Well, that and poop jokes, of course.

This story is a perfect example of how everything with Bunny has unfolded from the beginning. I set out trying to understand her, wind up going viral with Poo-Pourri, decide to research canine olfactory senses for more answers, and ultimately figure out that the only way to get over poop talk is to go deeper into poop talk.

It would have been easy to remove bunny's POOP button when she stopped using it to make a personal request to go out and started turning it into a tool to accuse Johnny and I of pooping in secret. Had I done that, I probably would have saved myself a good amount of embarrassment. But it's not up to me to control the way Bunny uses her buttons. It's up to me to give her more of them so she can tell me more about what she might want to say about the world around her. And that, my friends, is why I doubled down on POOP by adding a new button to her board: SMELL.

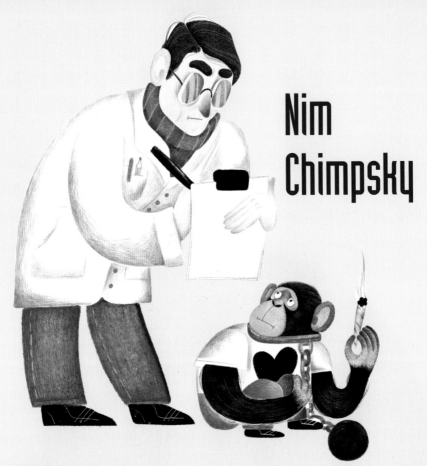

Nim Chimpsky

Herbert Terrace created a primate study in the 1970s that he dubbed Project Nim. The purpose of the study was to determine whether a chimpanzee could construct a sentence. The subject of the study was Nim Chimpsky, a chimp Herbert had cheekily named after Noam Chomsky, the linguist who famously stated that language was innate and unique to humans. Herbert aimed to prove Chomsky wrong with Project Nim.

Nim (who is one of the only characters in this story worth rooting for) did not have the best start. He was born in a primate research facility in Oklahoma. As an infant, he was pried screaming from the arms of his terrified mother, as all her previous babies had been. Terrace had recruited Stephanie LaFarge to become Nim's surrogate mother. She was a wealthy former student and lover of Terrace's who lived with her second husband, Weir, and seven kids in a brownstone in Manhattan. They were self-described "rich hippies," and not one of them knew sign language. In order to get Nim from Oklahoma to New York, Stephanie smuggled him on an airplane in a picnic basket. The flight attendants found out once they were in the air and brought the pilot out to see. Apparently Nim was cute enough that they let it slide. Can you imagine?

Back in New York, Nim would go to Columbia with Herbert during the day. He and a team of researchers would run cognition tests and teach Nim signs. Laura-Ann Petito was a cognitive neuroscientist and research assistant of Herbert's overseeing Project Nim, and one of the few people involved who actually had a working knowledge of American Sign Language. She was twenty at the time, and, oh yeah, she was Herbert's lover. He was forty.

At home in the brownstone, Stephanie's goals began to stray from that of Project Nim's. She was raising him as though he were her actual child. He slept in bed with her and she breastfed him. He was afforded as many freedoms as humanly possible. These included but were not limited to cigarettes, alcohol, and marijuana. He was, of course, not a human, but a wild chimpanzee. He was climbing the walls, establishing dominance, and expressing all sorts of innate chimpanzee behaviors that were not compatible with human family life.

After a brief stint in a country mansion owned by Columbia University, Nim was sedated and sent, unceremoniously, back to the Oklahoma research facility where he was born. He struggled to adjust, even in the presence of other chimps. The facility eventually fell on hard times, and Nim was sold to a pharmaceutical animal testing lab, where he lived in a small cage and was reported to have signed sadly to the other chimps there. Ultimately, he was purchased from the lab and lived the rest of his life at a horse sanctuary, where he died of a heart attack at the age of twenty-six.

After the data on Nim's life was analyzed, and after a lot of scientific back-and-forth, the ultimate conclusion was (sadly) that Nim never really learned to communicate effectively with sign language and that he was merely imitating his handlers. Ultimately, this wasn't a win for Terrace . . . but I don't think it was necessarily a win for Chomsky either. Honestly, I don't think there are any winners in this story. Terrace refers to what Nim did as "language 1"—unidirectional imperatives or requests to have basic needs met. For example, Nim's longest-ever sentence was, *Give orange me give eat orange me eat orange give me eat orange give me you.* According to Terrace, Nim never got to "language 2," which is conversational and conveys ideas above and beyond basic needs. For example, *Holy shit look at that sunset. Doesn't Washoe look beautiful in this light?* So, he kind of had language, it just wasn't human enough. But then again, the question of how language is defined is still up for debate. And it feels like we should've gotten that on lock before deciding to play dress-up with wild animals. Not just dress-up, either, but Little Orphan Ape. A huge cast of characters, endless traumas, and zero opportunity to live an authentic chimpanzee life. I'd have a hard time speaking too.

At the very least, a conversation is two-sided. A give-and-take. This experiment wasn't a conversation, but rather a monologue about power and ego. Terrace almost single-handedly dismantled the future of animal language studies, but for all the wrong reasons.

In the vast majority of animal language studies, the animals were taken out of their natural environment. In many cases, they were taken away from their parents during infancy and placed into a clinical setting with the sole purpose of teaching them to communicate with us, like us, initially guided by the idea that perhaps what was preventing communication was culture. Most of the animal language studies were performed with the intention of using what we learn to better understand ourselves. Some hypothesized that if apes were raised with humans, they would communicate like humans. Often, when the animal failed to succeed at the task at hand, they were abandoned to a life of testing, cages, and solitude. I'm thankful that the science I'm involved in is of the citizen variety, and with animals selectively bred for their excellent companionship and symbiotic relationship with humans.

9

How to Ask for Help

I've spoken to a lot of dog trainers and behavior consultants about reactivity and aggression, and there seems to be a couple of schools of thought on the difference between the two. Some believe that aggression is intent to harm, while reactivity is an aggressive display as a reaction to external stimuli. Others maintain that there's no real difference, they're different labels for the same set of behaviors, though there's certainly a whole lot more stigma attached to "aggressive" than there is to "reactive." Either way, people associate aggressive dogs with biting, but what many people don't realize is that the ladder of aggression starts with subtle de-escalation signals—like yawning, lip licking, or looking away. It's when those cues are missed—when no human intervenes to remove the trigger or the dog from the situation—that the reactive behavior escalates to biting.

I bring this up because Bunny started showing signs of reactivity just before she turned one. It looked to me, an inexperienced dog guardian, like an

aggressive overreaction to otherwise normal stimuli, such as new objects, dogs, and people—actually, let me rephrase that. I started recognizing signs of reactivity in Bunny just before she turned one. She'd quickly approach people and dogs she didn't know in a manner that I assumed was friendly, because at the time I didn't know enough about canine body language to be able to tell the difference. These approaches would culminate in a fairly terrifying display of barking and lunging. I learned pretty quickly that this wasn't one-off behavior and that we might have a problem. I hadn't known what to look for and wasn't prepared for what it meant because, like many first-time dog owners, I was under the misguided impression that a puppy was a blank slate full of endless potential and wonder, and that if I did everything right, she would become the perfect dog. And she is the perfect dog! She's a perfect sweet princess, and she's also reactive.

For all the talk about whether language acquisition is more nature or nurture, we must also look at that chicken and egg when talking about reactivity. Puppies are not tabulae rasae. You cannot create your dream dog no matter how well intentioned or well informed you are. You can, however, try to understand the genetic predispositions of the breed or breed mix you are bringing into your life and work with those predispositions. Canine behavioral studies over the last century have consistently shown that tendencies toward fearfulness, aggression, drive, impulsivity, and other traits are heavily influenced by breeding. But even so, there is a ton of genetic variation within breeds, so there is an element of unpredictability no matter what. So what I'm really saying here is that if you have a reactive dog, you're not alone, and it's probably not your fault. Additionally, if *you* are reactive, you're not alone, and it's not your fault. We are all products of our environment, learning history, and genetics.

Reactivity in dogs is an emotional response. More specifically, reactivity in dogs is an emotional response that has been deemed inappropriate by humans. An overreaction. Which makes sense, right? Barking, lunging, snapping, and attacking other dogs or humans is not ideal for cohabitation. Historically, many animals are punished for these displays. While this is understandable, it in no way treats the underlying emotions that often cause reactivity in the first place. These emotions could be anything: fear, frustration, insecurity, excitement. Basically, the same things that cause humans to lash out. Again, much like humans, the way canines respond to intense emotions or trauma can be boiled down to a few key responses: fight, flight, freeze, or fawn. The first three are fairly self-explanatory, but *fawning* can be harder to identify as a trauma response. Think of nervous laughter in a human. It doesn't imply that something is funny or that someone is having a good time. It's called "nervous" for a reason. I giggle when I watch horror movies not because I'm a psychopath, but because my fear response is to fawn in this instance. So what does fawning look like in our canine friends? It can look like pushy, over-the-top play solicitation, or in Bunny's case, she might approach a stranger in a soft wiggly manner that seems to say, "I am happy to meet you," when in fact she is afraid and fawning. This can quickly escalate to air snaps, growls, and lunging, so it's important to be aware of all the possible responses to fear.

For anyone out there with a reactive dog, here's the good news: over time, you can work to change your pet's emotional response to stimuli. I won't lie to you, it's not a process that happens overnight. But punishing a dog's reactivity is useless at best, tantamount to me saying," I'm scared" and someone responding, "Don't be. That's stupid." (Which is unfortunately something I have actually heard.) Humans are talented at emotional dismissal, and even humans whose job it is to be empathetic get it wrong. I once had a therapist fall asleep during our session while I was talking about an incredibly traumatic event. I called him on it, told him it made me angry, and he said it wasn't his fault because he'd been staying up late planning his vacation. I fired him. The

point is that hiding, burying, and invalidating emotions is not only ineffective, it leads to deeper trauma.

In humans, we hold traumatic experiences not just in our brains, but in our bodies as well. The physiological experience of "remembered" trauma leads us to believe that we are unsafe or even physically unwell when presented with our triggers, which can then be expressed both as behavior and illness. Unlike dogs, our behaviors don't usually include lip licking, yawning, or biting. In humans, triggers can immediately lead to panic, rage, fight or flight, and, in the longer term, can set off coping behaviors like eating disorders, addiction, dissociation, memory loss, anxiety, and depression, among others. Of course, these behaviors aren't always a response to trauma. But where there is trauma, one can usually find any number of these behaviors being used as tools to self-soothe and survive.

In theory, we're coming to understand these behaviors in other humans as a response to something, but it also feels like one of those things that the more we understand, the less we know. In practice, I see breakdowns in communication between strangers all day, every day, on social media, and even between friends and lovers, among whom one would assume the empathy is strong. Why, then, when dogs exhibit similar behaviors, do we still tend to label them as "bad"? Seems like "bad behavior" in dogs is really just behavior that's inconvenient for humans. I think about this a lot when I try to understand Bunny's reactivity.

I think it's important to focus on understanding behavior rather than labeling it. Not because I want to be on some high horse, but because that's what helped me recover from my own less-than-ideal reactive behaviors. I'll tell you a little bit about them, but this is a good spot for a quick trigger warning. If you're sensitive to content around eating disorders, skip the next three paragraphs.

I had an eating disorder for twenty-five years. I was hospitalized three times for a total of almost five months. It nearly killed me more times than I can count. A quarter of a century of self-loathing and terror so deep that it would have been easier to have starved or stuffed myself to death than learn to like myself. I had stopped taking note of days with no symptoms because that only led to disgust when I would inevitably relapse. Having been in my disorder for well over half of my life, I was convinced that my chances of recovery were nonexistent. The scientific literature seemed to corroborate this fear. What a downer, right?

Now I have almost four years with no symptoms under my belt (and I'll get into how that shift occurred in a bit), but previously I'd been incapable of caring for myself. Before recovery, I certainly wasn't in any position to care for a creature so entirely dependent on my choices. It was only after gaining some ground in recovery that I was finally ready, emotionally and physically, to welcome a dog into my life.

Gaining space from an active illness that had served as a crutch didn't mean that I had recovered from my trauma, but that I was ready to tackle it. Most days I'm still fifty-fifty on whether I believe my brain when it tells me we're okay, or my body when it tells me we're not, or vice versa—but I'm listening. If you're struggling with your own version of this stuff, I just want to remind you that you can't process trauma while you're in it, and you're not alone. Be kind to yourself.

While I suspect that not many people would actively choose a reactive dog as a pet, hear me out: reactive dogs can be therapists. I have never been forced to examine my own triggers and emotional responses as closely as I have with Bunny. I've found myself "antecedent, behavior, consequence–ing" myself in ways I never thought to do with my numerous human therapists. In theory, the ABCs of behavior are quite simple. The **A**ntecedent is the context or event that happens immediately before a behavior. The trigger. The **B**ehavior is what happens immediately after the trigger. And the **C**onsequence is the context or event that results from the behavior. The words *trigger* and *consequence* tend to hold negative connotations, but in this framework it helps to see them as neutral. For example, I ask Bunny to sit (antecedent); she sits (behavior); I give her a treat (consequence). Alternatively, fresh-baked pie is placed on the counter (antecedent); Bunny puts

her paws up to get a closer sniff and potentially a taste (behavior); I ask her to get off and cue her to lie down on her mat (consequence). And these pieces of learning theory apply universally to animals, human and nonhuman. A personal example: I make a to-do list (antecedent); I'm able to stay more focused and accomplish more in a day (behavior); I feel less anxiety (consequence).

Bunny has become the consummate therapist in more ways than one, without having to say a word—even though now she frequently does. Being self-tasked with the protection of Bunny's mental health has helped me to break big scary situations into tiny digestible pieces for both of us. I have a sense that we've both had the tendency to catastrophize, whether it be the sea gull on our deck or a flat tire. Neither of these things seem so big—in Bunny's case I can simply help her walk away from the window so she no longer has to see the evil featherhead, and in mine I can just call a friend and know that I'm not alone.

In another sense Bunny's my talk therapist too. Some of the things she asks remind me that there is so much left to learn and understand about ourselves and the world around us. One day last winter, both of us had something of a rough day. Bunny had been charged by both an off-leash puppy and an off-leash child. I'd had a doctor's appointment and an uncomfortable conversation with a colleague. I was watching Bunny from the dining room while she stood looking out the window. As though she could feel my eyes on her she turned around, walked to the board, and pressed FEEL ALL DONE FEEL ALL DONE. She walked over to me and put her head in my hands. It was a poignant reminder to me that expressing feelings is cathartic and that it's always okay to ask for help.

Of course, I'm not saying reactive dogs are like therapy dogs in the conventional sense, since true therapy dogs are known for being nonreactive and pretty much the exact opposite temperament to our Bunny. Therapy dogs are gentle and friendly with strangers, accept hugs, are seemingly unbothered by children, and provide comfort to a variety of individuals. Therapy dogs can be used to reduce symptoms of PTSD, anxiety, and depression. A type of comfort that we often associate with dogs in general is what we mean when we call them "man's best friend." This is what I innocently expected when I brought Bunny home. Turns out what I got instead was a therapist dog. One who challenges me; teaches me by modeling behaviors for self-advocacy, strength, resilience, and bravery; and that it's powerful to take your time. There's an adage that we get the dog we need, and in my case that's true. Bunny helps me break life's challenges into bite-size pieces. It's not easy—effective therapy can be tough sometimes, but that doesn't mean it's not worth it.

When I began working with Bunny, I hadn't even considered that my dog might be one of the challenging ones. I had the naive idea that the dogs that freak out must be the dogs without training or the dogs who have been mistreated. I now understand that this just is not true. Dogs, like people, are born with their own stuff. Their own psyches and struggles and pains, some of it purely innate. I want to talk about the grieving process people can go through when they learn they have a reactive dog. Often, I think we have an idea of who our dog will be. When reality doesn't align with our expectations, it can be a bit soul crushing. I've felt an exceedingly broad spectrum of emotions while coming to terms with Bunny's reactivity. Sorrow, guilt, frustration, resentment, pity, anger, empathy, confusion, resignation. Something akin to the feelings a mother might experience when they realize their human child isn't who they expected they'd be. Different interests, goals, lifestyle choices. And it's okay to have these feelings, provided we move through them with kindness.

At the same time, finding a way through it together is one of the most rewarding endeavors I've ever taken on. There are also incredible moments of pride when we have victories, and a feeling of deep compassion for what she's feeling as well as bottomless, truly unconditional love. And after all, that's what I was yearning for all along.

10

Tell Me How You Really Feel

et's talk about feelings, shall we?

When someone says that to me, I'm either in therapy or running in the opposite direction, so if you're still here, you get a cookie. Gregory Berns, a neuroscientist at Emory, trained dogs to lie still within an MRI scanner and mapped their brains—and guess what! Dogs and humans share all the same brain bits that produce emotions. Cognitive ethologist Marc Bekoff suggests that dogs are even capable of experiencing emotions that require more complex cognitive processing like shame, guilt, pride, and empathy. They're also capable of emotional contagion, which sounds kinda scary but really just means that they can easily identify and reciprocate our emotions. So yeah, Descartes, my fluffy potatoes do catch feelings.

I've had the word *anthropomorphization* thrown at me more times than I can count since I started sharing videos of Bunny online. At the beginning,

I was pretty careful to avoid comparing our feelings, but the longer I spend with her the more I realize that we are far more similar than we are different. Much of my time with Bunny has been spent drawing parallels between our experiences in an attempt at empathy. Primatologist Frans de Waal coined the term *anthropodenial*, which refers to discounting the emotional complexity of nonhumans. This, to me, seems far more dangerous. I can see it used as an excuse for inhumane treatment. What a disservice we do animals by not acknowledging our shared emotional experiences. If we are able to see our animal companions and ourselves as more alike than we are different, might we treat them with more compassion, patience, and respect? As I have begun, once again, to self-interrogate regarding my own emotional responses to triggers, I understand Bunny's with greater ease. I find empathy in spaces where before I may have been indifferent or even frustrated. Vulnerability feels more and more like a powerful tool than an admission of weakness.

Of all the emotions out there, love is the one I'd feel most justified in describing as unequivocally *good*, if I had to, although even love isn't without its comparative complications. The Greeks have a roster of words dedicated solely to various forms of love—from a love for mankind (Agape) to a love for friends and equals (Philia), and of course one for erotic love (Eros). The number of words the ancient Greeks had to represent love makes intuitive sense to me. Love may be a good feeling, but part of what makes it so complex is that there simply isn't one universal experience of it. Even *Merriam-Webster* provides nine possible definitions. This all tells us that love isn't simple. The definition of love that comes closest to the standard understanding of the feeling is "a strong affection." Describing love as a strong affection, while not inaccurate, seems almost too vague to be useful. Like defining community as "more than one person" or defining food as "something edible."

Love is something people know they're feeling because, well, they're feeling it. One of those "when you know you know" sort of things. Which is why I find it so confusing when I read comments like "That dog doesn't know what love is. That's a conditioned response." And while they might be right, they're also missing the point. It's possible that dogs don't understand the concept of love, and that any human who believes they do is just seeing canines through an anthropomorphic lens. On the other hand, if there's one thing we know for sure, it's that love doesn't exist on a binary scale. It would be tough to find two humans who have exactly the same definition and experience of love. In that sense, I don't think it's illogical to think that dogs could have their own experience of love as well.

So how do we prove love exists in dogs? Same way we prove anything: with science. So here's a chemical understanding of love. We've got testosterone and estrogen that play a part in lust. Dopamine, norepinephrine, and serotonin that feed attraction. And then my favorites: vasopressin and oxytocin that handle attachment. As it turns out, these chemicals aren't unique to humans. A 2015 study showed evidence of cross-species oxytocin release during periods of prolonged eye contact. Now, eye contact is a nuanced behavior among humans and an even more nuanced action among dogs. But if your furry friend is in a relaxed state and willing to gaze for a prolonged period of time into your eyes, it likely means that their brain is also being flooded with oxytocin, signaling that they too are experiencing attachment.

Anytime I am feeling particularly enamored with Bunny (which is most of the time), I'll walk over to the buttons with her and press LOVE YOU, then look into her eyes and wait for her to initiate the type of affection she desires most. Typically, that looks like her peering back into my eyes, placing her chin in my palm, and gently requesting ear rubs. I also model it every time I return from having been gone for a while. I'll walk through the door to see her wiggling bottom and open-mouthed smile, then promptly model HAPPY, LOVE YOU while

gleefully scritching her head in her favorite spot. So yeah, there may be some crossover between "love you" and "scritches," but it feels kinda the same as a hug or linking arms with your bestie.

So what "love you" means to both of us in these instances is that we are connected, both chemically and emotionally. And what it says about love in general is that it is not just a word or a feeling, but an active effort at connection built on trust. And that is the best definition of love that I've been able to come up with. Hearing those words from Bunny is confirmation that I've tried my best—that I'm good enough. Which is why, of all the word combinations Bunny has uttered, LOVE YOU MOM gets me the most.

11

The Monster Under the Bed Is Anxiety

The number of times that we've been alone in the house and Bunny has told me that we are, in fact, not alone has the potential to be its own horror movie. One evening in July 2020, Johnny was on a climbing trip, so it was just Buns and me. I was sitting on the couch, watching *Schitt's Creek*, when she approached the buttons.

Bunny: Mom.

Me: That's me. I'm Mom. What can I do for you?

Bunny: Stranger.

Me (*Skeptical. This isn't the first time she's been wrong about this.*)**:** Where? Where stranger?

She thinks for a good long time here, stares thoughtfully out the window, building suspense.

Bunny: Home.

Me: There's a stranger in the home?!

Bunny: Concerned. Upstairs.

Me (*Now also concerned, trying to keep my cool.*): Okay. Let's go upstairs and look for the stranger in the home.

We head upstairs, with me wishing I'd grabbed a kitchen knife just in case. We look in every room, under the bed, peek quickly into the closets, onto the deck. I breathe a sigh of relief and we head back downstairs.

Me: No stranger home. It's all good.

She looks right, then left, and pauses. Then goes back to her board of buttons.

Bunny: Oops.

Koko the Gorilla

Bunny is Gen Z's Koko.

—Instagram post

Koko is perhaps the most famous subject of all animal language studies, and as a kid who grew up in the 1980s and '90s, I've known about Koko for as long as I can remember.

Koko's caretaker was a woman named Francine "Penny" Patterson. She was a grad student in psychology at Stanford University. After Penny showed enough moxie to ask the San Francisco Zoo not once, but twice, to teach their newborn gorilla Koko sign language, they eventually relented, and Project Koko—had begun.

Within a week of working together, Koko was signing *food*, *drink*, and *more*. Oh, and I saved what might be the most baller Penny move for last: she didn't even know American Sign Language when she approached the San Francisco Zoo with this project idea. So she was learning alongside Koko, teaching herself as she went, trying to stay just one step ahead of her subject.

Project Koko ended up being the longest-running animal language study in history, spanning forty-four years and producing more than two hundred hours of footage, most of which has still never been released. At the time of her death, Koko was said to know around two thousand words of spoken English and one thousand signs in what Penny coined GSL (Gorilla Sign Language, an adapted version of ASL).

There are many parts of Koko's story that have raised ethical concerns over the years. I'm not going to lie to you, there's tea. We'll get into it, but I think it's important to remember that this is also a love story, one filled with dedication, education, controversy, and regret.

For the first two years of the project, Koko lived at the zoo and Penny would visit her daily. In 1974 she received permission from the zoo to take Koko to Stanford with her. You heard that right. They let a grad student take a baby gorilla to a university campus full time to teach it sign language out of a trailer where Koko lived. Wild times. When Koko was five, the zoo was like, "Hey, we need our gorilla back. It's time for her to make babies." But Penny was like, "Actually, here's twelve thousand five hundred dollars. She's my gorilla now."

I would be remiss if I failed to mention Allball—a tailless kitten that Koko chose from a litter and named herself. Koko wanted to be a mother, like she *really* wanted to be a mother, but it just never worked out. Penny has said that this is her greatest regret surrounding Project Koko. This extraordinarily tender relationship between a massive gorilla and a tiny kitten skyrocketed Koko's fame, and she began to make some pretty high-profile friends like William Shatner, Mister Rogers, Leonardo DiCaprio, Betty White, and Robin

Williams. The public notoriety helped the Gorilla Foundation secure funds and stay afloat.

Penny and Koko had two big years between 1978 and 1980. The Gorilla Foundation was moved from the Stanford campus to a new, permanent location in Woodside, California. An advisory board was formed for the foundation, one of whose members was Jane Goodall. And media clamored to cover the gorilla. Koko was on the cover of *National Geographic* magazine and featured on *60 Minutes*. A couple of documentaries were filmed about her. Oh, and Penny published her PhD dissertation: "Linguistic Capabilities of a Lowland Gorilla."

Even with all this highly public success, Penny and Koko weren't without their detractors. Penny responded to one paper titled "Why Koko Can't Talk" by saying, "My time would be much better spent conversing with gorillas," which we should all file away for future use.

Penny denied claims of inadvertent cueing and bias, of course, and presented evidence of uncued communications, like when Koko called a ring a *finger bracelet* and the time a volunteer was visiting Koko and had apparently overstayed their welcome. Koko signed "Time bye you," then when the volunteer responded "What?" Koko signed "Time bye goodbye." A straightforward gorilla after Bunny's own heart. And here's where things get particularly sticky for me as I begin to be able to see parallels in our journeys. I love Bunny like a child, and I'm fortunate to be in a position to spend all my time with her, exploring connection and communication. While I'm quite certain that most of our communications are uncued (that is, she starts them, and I follow suit), I think overinterpretation, bias, and projection are unavoidable. I'm human, in a deeply empathetic relationship with an animal whose communications I have to infer sometimes.

Penny and Koko were inseparable. They developed an extraordinary connection. One that even Penny describes as that of a mother and a daughter.

An interspecies relationship the likes of which had never been seen before. I can't imagine how challenging it must have been to remain unbiased to the extent that scientific rigor demands.

I feel quite lucky that within the research on animals and their use of buttons, I am tasked with nothing other than exploring the *what-if* and *why-not* of connection and communication with Bunny in whatever way I see fit. Record the data, send it to the scientists, and let them do the science. The thousands of us currently contributing data just get to understand our animals better. We become kinder captors, and maybe that empathy translates into a broader desire for understanding. As we have seen, hindsight is twenty-twenty, but I think we're moving in the right direction.

I have strong contradictory feelings when I look back at these early studies, and I think it's okay to feel two big things at once. Like I'm *really* trying to see the nuance, but unlike when I was a child filled with awe, I'm mostly left feeling quite uncomfortable. Penny herself has expressed regret at Koko's life not having been everything it could have been. On one hand, all these studies are inarguably exploitative. These were captive wild animals unable to exist as they should have (except, of course, the dogs). But if we're being honest, despite the fact that dogs are domesticated, they are still captive animals subject to our control and manipulation.

But there's the proverbial "other hand," which is this: These stories also inspired the world and showed millions that animals aren't machines. I don't care if Koko was literally talking. I don't care if it was "language." What she and Penny gave us was an understanding of the cognitive potential and emotional capacity of nonhumans. And maybe because of that we can sit for a moment in the idea that we're all just . . . well, animals experiencing the world in unique ways, desperate to be heard.

Make More Mistakes

Some days, most of what Bunny says speaks for itself. Other days, it feels like babble, or at least requires more interpretation than I'm comfortable with. Although she uses the buttons entirely of her own volition, I can see frustration when she is clearly trying to express something and I'm just not getting it. My inexperience with AAC and my relative newness to the world of animal communication and cognition has me frequently wondering if I'm moving too fast or in the wrong direction.

Kathy Sdao is an applied animal behaviorist extraordinaire who has also worked in language acquisition studies, specifically with dolphins. I first met up with her after I'd begun noticing some behaviors in Bunny that I didn't understand or know how to manage, specifically reactive behaviors toward strangers. We talked quite a bit about the work I was doing with the buttons too. She was surprised at how fast I'd moved with Bunny. In her work with

dolphins, she'd always adopted an "errorless learning" protocol, which is a type of positive reinforcement that sets your learner up for as much success and as little failure as possible by breaking behaviors down into tiny slices. For example, if I place two toys in front of Bunny and my goal is for her to be able to select the toy on the left when I say "Left get it," I'm going to start with just one toy, placed in front of and to the left of her. Provided she already knows "get it," she will have a 100 percent success rate, which equals more reinforcement and less frustration. Less frustration means longer, more successful training sessions that end up being more fun. After some successful reps of that, I'll add another toy, maybe of lesser value and placed farther away on her right so that the likelihood of her choosing the toy on the left is still very high. And so it goes. Classical conditioning is happening all the time, so building a bulk of positive associations by winning the game makes sense.

I wasn't nearly a skilled-enough trainer at the time to be successful at developing an errorless learning protocol with the buttons, and truthfully, not knowing what it was, I hadn't even considered it. I was familiar with trial-and-error learning. I do think many dogs are capable of handling a bit more frustration than we give them credit for, and that making mistakes is an important part of the learning process—at least, it has been for me. Errors are simply information. They let us know that we are moving too fast or haven't dissected the criteria enough. My small failures have encouraged me and Bunny to think creatively and solve problems. I felt like I understood how much frustration Bunny could handle. Just enough, and she'd be inspired to explore and try new tactics; too much, and she'd lose interest. If I continued to reward the same behaviors without upping the ante, I would get the same results. And it seemed to work. Bunny wasn't deterred by seemingly nonsensical exploration. She'd press new buttons immediately when they were added to the board, and with a smile seem to ask, "What's this one mean?"

Shaping has played a huge role in our training. Shaping is a process wherein you reward successive approximations of a desired behavior until arriving at the end result. It builds confidence and creates a problem-solving dog. For example, say I want to train Bunny to push a ball with her nose. I might start by marking and rewarding the exact moment she looks at the ball. By keeping the marker (either a clicker or the word *yes*) as precise as possible, Bunny has information about what behaviors are working. So maybe next time she looks at and moves toward the ball, I mark and reward that. Then perhaps she puts her paw on the ball. I'll mark and reward that because she's experimenting and getting closer to our goal. Next time she uses her paw, I'll wait and see if she offers something else, and, lo and behold, she boops the ball with her nose. I mark and reward, and so on and so forth. Because timing is important here, it increases clear communication as a handler. You really have to pinpoint the moments of success. Additionally, since there is no lure, phasing out treats becomes a nonissue. Most importantly, you get to see lightbulb moments, which resonate as huge successes for both the human and the dog. I've found these types of exercises invaluable in developing our connection, communication, and team-work. Shaping has always been easy for Bunny—she seems to love the challenge of it. Even when I was so much clumsier at training than I am today, she was all smiles when we were shaping. Thank goodness for her patience with me.

One of the challenges we face—well, I face—is encouraging fuller sentences from Bunny. In the famous words of Kevin from *The Office*, "Why waste time say lot word when few word do trick?" What would Bunny's impetus be to say, "I want beach walk now" when she knows perfectly well that simply pressing BEACH will likely get the same reaction? I have a few different approaches to this. One is consistently modeling longer sentences. If she presses BEACH, I'll join her at the board and model BUNNY WANT BEACH or another similar phrase. Sometimes when she presses BEACH and I'd like a bit more exploration, I'll remain silent, as I might in a shaping exercise, which may nudge her to repeat or elongate. Whatever her next utterance is, I'll reward contextually for her effort so she doesn't get so frustrated she stops trying to communicate. Another approach that I've explored has been slowly shifting the positions of some of the buttons toward her so that they form a sort of semicircle console. I imagine myself as an astronaut—I'd want all of my switches, buttons, and controls easily within reach. If I had to move too far from one end to the other, I'd likely not use the outliers as much.

I presume that not having enough words to explore could be almost as frustrating as having too many, and so I've tried to walk that line carefully. But again, I'm really just making it up as I go. As long as Bunny continues to enjoy the process, I don't see much of a need to follow an outside protocol that wasn't designed specifically for us. I think that's one of my favorite parts: feeling like we are really able to experiment as we figure this all out together.

Bunny and I have some things in common in this regard. We are both independent, but highly motivated by praise when it's coming from the right source. We both have strong opinions and don't appreciate unsolicited advice. We are more likely to comply when we are *asked* to do a thing and not *told* to do a thing. We both appreciate a challenge. We are both sensitive to subtle cues, and I think because of these similarities we've been able to forge an unusual path together. Lots of give and take, plenty of mistakes, tons of laughter, and unyielding love.

THE ACCIDENTAL POET

Bunny's explorations of her board often feel like poetry to me. She plays with novel word combinations and her phrases have a style and rhythm that I certainly didn't teach her.

BUNNY'S MORNING HAIKU:

Come poop walk poop now
Morning hmmm help go poop Mom
Did potty see more

BUNNY'S AFTERNOON HAIKU:

Today afternoon
Night go stranger animal
Yesterday before

BUNNY'S EVENING HAIKU:

Who this help concerned
I human we family
Why this where love you

13

Comfort Chameleon

've long believed that I'm not qualified to do something amazing, and that my options are limited by what I can fool people into believing I am capable of. I think a lot of this stems from an educational path that was a bit unconventional. I'm not college educated. I only completed two years of "real" high school. I homeschooled myself through graduation because, well, high school sucks (at least it did for me). I couldn't find a way to navigate painful social anxiety, understimulating classes, and a debilitating eating disorder simultaneously without self-destructing.

I went to five different high schools, two of which were in Italy. I was there for my junior year, and in the first six months I experienced the continuation of a long string of traumas that I've struggled to recover from ever since. That's when the eating disorder really took hold, although I believe that the road there had been paved long before. I didn't do much (any) textbook learning while I was there. I learned a language, I learned a culture, and I learned some things about myself. My credits weren't transferable when I came home, but the thought of repeating a year gave me panic attacks, so I forged my transcripts in Italian, did a couple of months of senior year at a public high school, then removed myself to complete my credits and diploma through an independent studies program. I often wonder if I'm a loner because of this or in spite of this. I never went to prom or had a friend group. I lived in the woods, and before the internet was a thing, I spent the majority of my time reading books, exploring, and daydreaming. I am ever resistant to asking for help, remain independent to a fault, and have, for the majority of my life, considered myself a social and academic failure.

What I didn't realize is that the vast majority of education happens outside of school, bolstered by curiosity and a desire to know a little about a lot, and a lot about a few things. Bunny is an education, and with a steep learning curve at that. Some of her lessons I've been altogether unprepared for, but when we stop learning, we turn into assholes who think we know better than everyone else, so I generally try to remember that I don't know shit in the grand scheme of things.

Testing a lot of professional hats over the years became my normal, mostly because I become bored easily, but also because I don't like being told what to do. I've been a ballroom dance instructor, a sake sommelier, and a personal assistant working out of my boss's home. That last job ended abruptly when I realized my in-home office had been newly decorated with a giant oil painting of a penis sporting angel wings, hovering over a white picket fence. I've worked in a dozen restaurants, from Korean mom-and-pop, to diner, to French fusion, and Japanese fine dining. All these jobs taught me valuable lessons, and I would become really good at a thing for a time. But the main lessons are that I am not built to work for someone else, and if I am bored, I will fail, often catastrophically.

My last day of working for a business that wasn't my own was sometime in early 2017. It was around that time that I started designing wearable art. I'd been a maker and an artist for as long as I can remember, but had flitted from one practice to another as I lost interest or inspiration. This felt different. There was a strong purpose and deep emotional connection to what I was producing. Imagine armor, chain mail and scales—but instead of a medieval bent, think contemporary and future fashion. Something that one could wear as metaphorical protection from the world at large, allowing one to be their most authentic self. "Armor for those that dream of vulnerability" became my business's tagline, adopted from the feedback of countless collaborators and from my own personal experience of wearing it.

As my business grew, I had the opportunity to work with tons of amazing artists. We were doing photo shoots every week, I was lucky enough to grace the cover of many small magazines, was featured in music videos and film, showed twice at New York Fashion Week, and was selected at Paris Fashion Week as a "best street style" contender. My pieces were available in several boutiques. I had found my community and a passion and, by extension, found myself. And almost imperceptibly, my struggles with food started to fade into the background, until one day I realized that I had slipped into recovery without even noticing that it had happened. I felt proud of myself for the first time. Ever. My body relinquished its long-held and precious crutch, meaning that I was safe enough to be human again. To feel and connect. My new armor and my life tools were art, independence, and authenticity. This created space for new emotional exploration and a renewed drive to connect.

Then, in 2020, the COVID-19 pandemic hit. People suddenly weren't in the market for wearable art. Boutiques shuttered. Live events were indefinitely canceled. Online sales slowed. Fashion shows and photo shoots were no more. But I would be okay. I'd need to hustle a bit harder, but I'd be fine. I thought it'd be a couple of months, but before we knew it it'd been three years. A few months in, I began to recognize the gravity of the situation, and while business was still trickling in, my focus began to shift more completely . . . to my new dog.

Bunny kept me sane.

For me, more free time amounts to more anxiety. So I redoubled my efforts with Buns, finding connection without judgment with her to be my safe space. We spent our days getting to know each other, studying each other's behaviors, exploring different ways to communicate, playing, complex problem-solving, and tenderly adapting to one another's quirks. I found this practice grounding and humbling. I'd placed myself for so long at the bottom of some sort of mental and emotional hierarchy, and now having found partnership within an entirely different species, I realized that we are all the same.

14

Animal
Polyglot?

ooking for a precise definition of language has proven to be confounding, because it seems there isn't one. Its primary purpose of course is to facilitate communication. This much is universally agreed upon. But I suppose the way that it is most commonly defined as uniquely human is by suggesting that other animals lack infinite productivity and creativity in their communicative styles. But to me this just seems like another anthropocentric way of saying "humans number one," and given ongoing interest and research into how other animals communicate and into their "languages," it's clear that it's a fascinating topic and one we don't know nearly enough about. It's ludicrous to claim that the way we communicate is the be-all and end-all. Staying humble enough to recognize that we don't know everything is not one of humanity's strong suits. And even though I can find creativity in Bunny's utterances, I'm not saying that she is actually writing poetry, making puns, or creating riddles. But has she? Could she? She's certainly made some poop jokes, right?

That said, I never realized how weird and complicated English was until I started trying to teach it to my dog. I studied Russian in school and spent some time in Russia, became proficient in Italian while I lived in Naples, and had a working understanding of "restaurant Japanese" from my time spent in Japanese fine dining—but still, I'd never really thought about it. I feel like languages, and certainly accents, have always come pretty naturally to me, particularly through immersion. And now that I've been exposed to other methods of communication, I wonder how my interactions with the world are changing.

I find myself wondering whether Bunny learning to communicate with buttons could have fundamentally changed the way she tackles communication, not just with humans but also with other dogs. Does she perhaps expect more from them? Does she expect other dogs to proceed as thoughtfully as she does, or does she expect extended focus from other humans? Has closing the communication gap become fulfilling in its own right to her?

I know that when I was ballroom dancing, I began to really analyze nonverbal communication more than I ever had before, and I could tell whether or not someone was assertive within the first step of a closed-hold waltz. And learning other languages made me more aware of the idiosyncrasies of my own. When I returned from Italy, I had forgotten the English word *popsicle* and had to resort to calling it an "ice juice stick." Our brains literally change through immersive anything—language, trauma, positive reinforcement—so it would make sense to me that Bunny's perception of the world might differ from that of other dogs, although there is no way of knowing for sure.

A study in 2014 from researchers at the University of Sussex in England determined that canines and humans process speech in very much the same way. They are able to distinguish between meaningless and meaningful sound sequences, processing the meaning of words in the left hemisphere and emotional meanings in the right, then combining the two.

Other studies have shown that bilingualism helps executive function in humans and correlates with denser gray matter in the brain, particularly in the prefrontal cortex, which is responsible for advanced processing. Bilingualism has also been shown to slow cognitive decline. Could Bunny's brain physiologically be changing in a way that allows for a greater understanding of language? Is she thinking in swirling graphic sentences, but only able to express dotted lines? There is an unconscious process that speakers partake in constantly, thinking about what to say, formulating how to say it, then articulating it. Contemplating all this as a part of Bunny's process makes it even more wondrous.

The word *run* has hundreds of meanings. Bunny runs the show. She's spicy, and it runs in the family. She gets recognized when we run errands, and the account I run on Instagram shows our adventures and her run-on sentences. See what I mean?

The philosophy of language is a topic, as complicated and enigmatic as it is, that has its own annual conferences. Not to be confused, of course, with the philosophy of linguistics and its annual membership meetings. Now, I don't even want to pinky touch an explanation of these two areas of study other than to say that philosophy of language examines the origins and nature of language and the relationship between meaning and truth, while philosophy of linguistics examines the relationship between language, its users, and the world. Philosophy itself exists because of our inability to make sense of something, which furthermore illustrates that shit is crazy.

One of the most influential philosophers of the twentieth century was Ludwig Wittgenstein. He coined the term *language games*. Essentially, he stated that language isn't stable and directly representational but living and multidimensional. That

in order to learn language, one must use it. That the rules of language mean nothing without also playing the game, and that context is what gives words meaning. Context is the rule of the game. For instance, the word *outside* could be a question, a demand, or an observation. Bunny's game and my game aren't exactly the same, but we learn each other's rules as we grow together, developing our own game—in essence, our own language, both with and without words.

I wonder what Noam Chomsky and B. F. Skinner would have to say about this. Ah yes, the age-old debate. Is language learned (as Skinner said) or is it innate (as Chomsky claimed)? As with most great debates, the truth likely lives somewhere in the middle.

My interpretations of Bunny's button presses are informed by her history of responses, as is the way I find myself talking to her. It's a mutualistic and self-fulfilling relationship. For example, I now say "play poop" instead of "fart" when talking to her, because it's a term she coined, and I therefore adopted. Similarly, I say "sound settle" or "settle sound" to mean "be quiet," because she uses those combinations frequently in that context. Sometimes when I talk to her, my syntax is off because I will have understood her meaning, and I forget that there is a more precise pattern that I could be following.

I wasn't truly aware of this until the other day, when I was on my weekly call with Leo and Federico at UCSD. One clip I sent to them recently played out this way:

Bunny: *Come love you mom bye*

Me: Come love you mom bye? Where do you want to go?

Bunny: *Friend*

Me: Go play friend? We did play Tango before. Maybe after my meeting we can play Beacher.

Bunny walks to the window and looks in the direction of Beacher.

My responses during this interaction were fast and clear. I understood exactly what she was trying to say and didn't hesitate. It wasn't so clear to Federico, however. He asked how I had interpreted her initial utterance, to which I said, "Well, she was telling me sweetly that she needed my attention because she wanted to go somewhere"—*come* (come here), *love you* (please), *bye* (let's go). I hadn't even given it a second thought because she had used these sorts of phrases contextually so many times before.

"Ahhhh," said Federico, "this could be an example of ontogenetic ritualization."

"Oh, totally," I said . . . then realized I had no idea what he was talking about. "What does that mean?"

"Ontogenetic ritualization. When you converge to a code between two individuals who interact frequently with each other and that others might not immediately understand," he explained.

"Oh, that actually makes a ton of sense," I responded.

Evidence of this has been studied in the great apes, and I would posit that Bunny and I have developed our own language game. People who have followed us for a while on social media begin to understand it and can play the game as well, while to some it may appear mostly nonsensical, particularly when viewed outside of context. This is what I love most about language, and perhaps why it is so enigmatic. It is constantly evolving with culture and tradition, nuanced in a million different ways within every relationship. Language is personal, powerful, productive, and creative. And without saying that Bunny is using language, I can certainly say that how she uses words is personal, powerful, productive, and creative. So, if it's not really "language," well . . . who cares?

Bias Is Unavoidable

Do I contradict myself?
Very well then I contradict myself.
(I am large, I contain multitudes.)

—*Walt Whitman*

I've loved this quote by Whitman for as long as I can remember. It's a brilliant reminder that, without questioning our own truths, we cease to grow. We are allowed to change our minds. We are allowed to change the entirety of our being as often as we need to, in order to continue evolving. There is a huge emphasis, in American culture at least, on sticking to one's beliefs and taking pride in one's personal opinions. And while I agree with the importance

of this, I also think that the inability to allow those opinions and beliefs to advance has led to wild polarization and ideological extremes.

I change my mind all the damn time. I have to—whether it's rerouting my inner monologue or adding new information to my knowledge base that changes everything I thought before. This is how we as a species do better. In fact, by the time this book comes out, I'll likely have changed my opinions several times over.

During one of my many hospitalizations for anorexia and bulimia, it was suggested that I suffered from alexithymia—which, in my starved delirium, I assumed was named after me. Alexithymia is essentially emotional color blindness and is defined by several factors. The one that speaks most to my experience is difficulty identifying feelings and distinguishing between feelings and the bodily sensations of emotional arousal. What this means for me specifically is that when I experience a "large" emotion, even given a seemingly obvious context, I find it difficult to label. And this isn't just about differentiating between, say, frustration and rage, or contentment and glee. I often won't even be able to tell if it lies on a conventionally positive or negative spectrum. It's very confusing and can take an inordinate amount of introspection for me to sort it out. It's considered a personality construct, and although it isn't a core feature of autism spectrum disorder, there is significant overlap. In fact, one study published by the National Library of Medicine suggested that up to 20 percent of persistent eating disorders may in fact be undiagnosed autism.

They threw a ton of potential diagnoses at me, but most of them didn't stick. Read as, "Here's a prescription for Lexapro and a hamburger." I think they were just frustrated that they couldn't easily fix me, but it is true that I've never felt neurotypical. I sometimes can't recognize what I'm feeling without lengthy self-analysis, so it tracks that my opinions undulate, and sometimes I don't trust them at all.

I believe that the amount of time I've had to dedicate to understanding

and recognizing my own emotions has made me more sensitive to the feelings of those around me—well, that and a healthy dose of trauma, but that's an entire other book. In my relationship with Bunny, I believe this awareness and hypersensitivity has made me markedly more tuned in to her subtle cues. In fact, exploring how she may experience emotions has in turn helped me to analyze my own. I wonder if, given my proximity to her emotional world, I could ever remain as unbiased as some people claim I ought to be in interactions with Bunny. This feels not only unnecessary but impossible, which brings me to some biases that I've become conscious of in trying to examine my own. Because when we're not critically examining our own biases and beliefs we're unlikely to be able to sit in the nuance necessary to even have discussions like this.

Have you ever thought you were really good at something or knew a lot about it, until you learn more, only to realize that you're not as much of an expert as you thought? This is known as the Dunning-Kruger effect, and it basically states that our ignorance is invisible to us. It's a type of cognitive bias in which people grossly overestimate their competence in a specific area due to a lack of self-awareness. Justin Kruger and David Dunning stated in 1999: "Those with limited knowledge in a domain suffer a dual burden: Not only do they reach mistaken conclusions and make regrettable errors, but their incompetence robs them of the ability to realize it."

While I have likely fallen victim to this at times in my life, I hope not so much within my work with Bunny. If anything, I'm more prone to succumb to the Dunning-Kruger effect's polar opposite—impostor syndrome. This is when you never feel deserving of success, are plagued by self-doubt, and constantly feel like a fraud waiting to be outed. This has been my biggest challenge while writing this book. *No one wants to hear what I have to say. I don't know what I'm talking about. Word salad. Blah.* Perhaps because of this I feel overly conscientious of the risk of cognitive bias and the "Clever Hans effect."

Hans was a horse in the early twentieth century that was thought to be able to perform amazing feats of reading, spelling, and arithmetic, but was found by psychologists to be simply responding to inadvertent cues from audiences and his trainer. Still an amazing feat, just not what we thought it was. My awareness of the Clever Hans effect, however, doesn't altogether protect me from it or the multitude of unavoidable biases that just exist in us because of culture, experience, or genetic makeup. Biases come from a place of self-preservation. They are cognitive shortcuts meant to aid in survival, and when viewed through that lens, I don't see how I couldn't be biased in most aspects of life.

Imagine Neanderthals having no bias toward or against saber-toothed tigers. Probably ends well for the tiger and not so well for the caveperson. We have biologically preinstalled biases to keep us alive. But then we add biases on top of those from our learning history. We have explicit biases that we are consciously aware of, like the fact that I don't care for cherry-flavored candy. We also have implicit biases that are expressed subtly and unconsciously and that with careful introspection we may become aware of. Racism is one such example. Many isms fall into this category, finding themselves there after long, messy cultural obfuscations of mythology or religion.

Science attempts to eliminate bias so that we can arrive at objective truth. Bias threatens transparency and logic, right? But bias-free science does not exist. In fact, basic presuppositions are the foundational premises of science. Our carried philosophical assumptions implicitly influence how we analyze the world. So when someone says Bunny's conversations are all cognitive bias on my part, I say, "Probably! Let's discuss!" because that's some pretty interesting stuff. But it's not the zinger they think it is.

Kanzi

Of all the animals listed in these profiles, Kanzi the bonobo is the only one still with us at the time of writing. Sue Savage-Rumbaugh worked with Kanzi for four decades. He was born on October 28, 1980, at the Yerkes Field Station at Emory University in Atlanta, Georgia. He wasn't the initial focus of her studies, though. At the time of his birth, Sue had been trying to teach Yerkish (a lexigram language consisting of a keyboard or laminated pages containing symbols that correspond to objects and ideas) to Kanzi's adopted mother, Matata. Kanzi was always in the room when they trained but wasn't part of the lessons.

When Kanzi was two, Matata was taken away for breeding, and he was devastated. That first day, Savage-Rumbaugh noted that he used the keyboard more than three hundred times, of his own volition, to request food, affection, and to ask where his mother was. He had learned as a human baby does, through observation. Sue realized that social communication was key and that paying special attention to what animals might want to communicate about and giving them those opportunities was crucial to successful communication. Kanzi became the focus of her work, and by the time he was five he'd been on the front page of the *New York Times*. He now knows over three thousand spoken words and uses more than three hundred fifty symbols to communicate.

Like Dr. Pepperberg, Sue's team employed rigorous controls to ensure there would be no inadvertent cueing. In early tests, Sue would wear a welder's mask and avoid any gestures while asking Kanzi to perform a series of random tasks like "Put the pine needles in the refrigerator," "Get the ball that's outside," and "Put on the monster mask to scare Linda." And he performed nearly every request without hesitation. But Harvard psychologist Steven Pinker was unimpressed, equating these acts to a bear riding a unicycle in a Moscow circus.

William Fields, a senior research scientist and director of scientific research at the Great Ape Trust, claims that Kanzi demonstrated *theory of mind*, which is the ability to understand another individual's perspective. He was missing a finger, and Kanzi, while holding Fields's hand, noticed the missing finger and used his keyboard to say "hurt." He also speaks of bonobo vocalizations that, over time, came to resemble English words, which acoustic analysis seemed to confirm. These humans and apes had developed a unique culture that allowed for never-before-seen behaviors and communications.

This story, like any story of a captive wild animal, is not without its ethical complications. When the Ape Initiative took over the Great Ape Trust in 2013, it fell on them to help Kanzi lose seventy-five pounds after his health and that of the other seven bonobos in their care had allegedly been neglected.

Prior to the transition, Sue had been put on administrative leave as director of the Great Ape Trust after allegations from twelve former employees (researchers and primatologists) that she was unfit to care for the bonobos. A US Department of Agriculture inspection found the facilities in good condition, and Sue was reinstated after the charges were investigated by the board and found to be "baseless and unsubstantiated."

Despite drama seeming to be the norm in these stories, Sue is recognized for tremendous accomplishments. She published seven books and 170 research papers. In 2011, she was recognized as one of the one hundred most influential people in the world by *Time* magazine. She too had criticisms of prior animal language studies. At a symposium in 1974, she stated that by focusing on sign language, researchers failed to take into account the apes' natural gestural and vocal communications. It was after this that she was offered a job working with bonobos.

The Ape Testimony Project offers a unique, firsthand account of what that was like from the perspective of Sue herself and several people who worked closely with her. Ultimately, she was removed from research through the Ape Initiative, as their goals and research protocols changed. She hasn't been allowed contact with Kanzi or any of the other bonobos with whom she was close since, despite the fact that the bonobos repeatedly ask for her. Another heartbreaking end to what was quite obviously a deep and loving connection.

16

Why Dog?

n the fall of 2020, a meme went viral in which people acted as if they were Bunny going through an existential crisis. There are thousands of them. There was even an article in Junkee examining the phenomena.

The inspiration: Bunny had begun using her WHY button to seemingly question the mundane responses I repeatedly give to her. "I love you," I'd say.

"Why?" Bunny would reply.

Then just a few days later, she looked at herself squarely in the mirror and pressed WHO THIS followed by HELP and CONCERNED. Not once, but twice, in the space of a week.

The vast majority of the memes were lighthearted and fun, but a surprising number of them seemed created out of genuine terror.

One such video plays out like this: A person pretending to be Bunny stares wide-eyed and open-mouthed at the camera and pretends to push buttons saying, "Bunny. Have. Rights. Hmmm?" Cut to the same person pretending to be me: "John, we don't even have a rights button. The dog made a button."

Another one starts with a woman facing the screen saying through nervous laughter, "Ha ha ha! It's all fun and games. Bunny's becoming more sentient. But what happens when Bunny one day goes: 'Why. Bunny. Mamma. Friends. If. Mamma. Own. Bunny. Hmmmmm?'"

Yet another features a redhead smiling and saying, "Hey Bunny, wanna go for a walk?" The same person as Bunny says, "Bunny is God hmmmm?" Looking concerned, the first speaker says, "How . . . how about treat?" Bunny says, "Bunny could kill God hmmmm?"

All of them begs the question: Why does the idea of a dog with self-awareness make people so uncomfortable? Is it the inevitable canine uprising à la *Planet of the Apes* that people fear? Or is it more of a "how dare these fluffy potatoes have complex internal lives because if they do then I'm a bad person for not recognizing it" kind of scenario?

René Descartes, the seventeenth-century mathematician and philosopher, the man who gave us "I think therefore I am," held that animals cannot reason or feel pain or pleasure, and that they are ostensibly soulless machines. He said that only humans have minds, can learn and have language, and therefore only humans are deserving of compassion. And to prove this point, he violently tortured his wife's dog, and many others, cutting them open while still alive, to literally poke at their hearts and marvel at their painless existence. A continued moral indifference to the welfare of animals that I fear we still haven't gained as much distance from as we ought to have.

As horrifying and absurd as this is to any animal lover, it wasn't until 2008 (let that sink in for a sec) that the idea of animal sentience was brought into law, with the Treaty of Lisbon officially acknowledging the sentience of animals and requiring full regard to their welfare in the EU.

So, back to this meme. It seems a fear born entirely out of ego. A human inability to release a long-held, but inaccurate, belief that humans are the in-tellectually, morally, and emotionally superior species. This antiquated belief is made more difficult to let go of because of the very human challenge we face when trying to legally define sentience. But this doesn't have to be so hard. I mean, even the Supreme Court, when confronted with something difficult to define that was much less important than a life, has concluded "I know it when I see it"—Justice Potter Stewart's threshold for obscenity. A thing without clearly defined parameters, but instantly recognizable nonetheless.

Progress is progress, I suppose. And the fact that animal consciousness makes people uncomfortable means, at the very least, that they are thinking about animals in a way that may lead to better treatment of them. I for one have always assumed that animals possess rich emotional capacity, and that although they most certainly experience the world in ways quite different from ourselves, we are more similar in our curiosities, in our suffering, and in our joy than we have been led to believe.

Why This?

One of Bunny's utterances that really sticks out to me is WHY THIS?

It wasn't said in an existential sense. I'd woken her up from a nap to ask if she wanted to go to the park, to which she responded, "Why this?" It's a phrase that I come back to time and again throughout this journey. From the beginning, I've been bombarded by opinions, questions, criticism, and appreciation. It's a lot, both positive and negative, and I've frequently found it difficult to remain unaffected by all these outside influences.

There are too many buttons, you're confusing her.

Just let her be a dog.

She doesn't ever seem happy.

In moments like these, I too ask, "Why this?" Sometimes my answers to these questions aren't clear-cut, but the underlying theme when it comes to Bunny and me has unwaveringly remained—connection.

Exploring new ways of communication with Bunny has allowed me to examine the way I communicate with the world, and also with myself. I am more

in awe of the power of words than ever before, and I now realize how I've taken for granted my ability to communicate. It's a marvel that we are able to express an infinite number of wild and wonderful thoughts, and for as much effort as I have put into understanding Bunny aside from the buttons, there are things about her that I simply wouldn't know if we hadn't chosen this path together.

Bunny's reward, like mine, is both being and feeling connected and understood. In all honesty, I think I communicate better with Bunny than with anyone else in my life. Johnny is 100 percent my person, but there is a different quality to my relationship with Bunny. Perhaps it's because she's my dependent, and perhaps it's because Johnny and I have too many words and sometimes they get in the way. But one thing above all is for sure: it's about an inherent shift in my desire to really understand. Now, whenever anyone is speaking, I find myself slowing down, focusing, and listening with more compassion and openness than I have in the past. Bunny has also taught me to question the limits of what is possible—and that is spreading. I can see these ways of listening and being and thinking moving through the community. People are paying attention.

It doesn't matter what the results are of the scientific study we participate in, or any future study, because the way people look at animals is fundamentally shifting. To me, the truth is simple: Our animals have been talking to us all along, we just haven't been listening. So even if our "why" and the "this" are ever changing, the constants of love and respect should remain the guiding principles.

18

Alpha Schmalpha

People have told me my whole life that I should meditate, that yoga will help with my anxiety. "Like, it seriously changed my life," they'd say. But when I try, I just find myself furiously bored, enraged by how thoroughly I feel I'm wasting my time. Also, someone telling me that I should do something is a surefire way to dissuade me from doing that very thing. I don't think I'm stubborn necessarily; just don't tell me what to do. A request offered with positive reinforcement is the safest bet. This, in turn, is how I've approached training with Bunny from day one.

My tattoo artist and I were finishing up some work on my sleeve the other day and she referred to me as an alpha personality. I've never even remotely considered myself alpha, but it did get me thinking.

In 1947, Rudolph Schenkel—a Swiss animal behaviorist—published a study after watching wolves in captivity, which gave rise to the now outmoded "alpha" theory. Several years later, in 1970, L. David Mech—a wildlife research biologist—published *The Wolf: Ecology and Behavior of an Endangered Species*, which further perpetuated the idea that wolves compete through dominance to establish hierarchy. Put simply, "the biggest bully wins." But then, in 1990, after many years studying wolves in their natural environment, Mech published a new paper, "Leadership in Wolf *Canis Lupis* Packs," that drastically changed his position. He proposed that wolf packs operate as a familial unit—similar to humans—and thus the elders/breeding pair in the pack make the guiding decisions for the rest of the pack, who are their offspring. And just like most familial units, they quarrel, but also share affection, attachment, and play. They help each other. Mech has since pleaded with his publisher to discontinue publication of his earlier work, to no avail, and unfortunately, dominance theory in dog training is still surprisingly prevalent.

A 2010 study of wild Italian pack dogs, conducted at the University of Parma by Roberto Bonanni, found that even larger packs, including several families, will share leadership roles among the elders based on the particular strengths that the individual has to contribute to the welfare of the pack. In fact, rather than the strongest and most dominant dogs attaining a leadership role, it seems that the friendliest, most social, and most capable of keeping the peace tend to rise to power. It's a whole *culture* that has been systematically dismissed by human ineptitude and myopia as "alpha" until pretty recently. The notion of human "alphas" is just as much a fallacy, and far more dangerous. It's a pseudoscientific excuse for bad behavior and bullying in those recklessly grasping at power.

Here is the problem with dominance theory in dog training. First and foremost, it creates an adversarial relationship. We as humans are really terrible at reading and responding to the subtleties of canine body language. Dominance theory would have us mimic the aggressive tactics seen in unrelated wolves forced together into captivity in an attempt to be the leader of a pack that doesn't exist. We are not a pack. We are (hopefully) cohabitating peacefully and voluntarily. And our attempt to mimic this false idea of how wolf packs

function is made sillier by the fact that even if we wanted to believe this about wolves, dogs aren't wolves. There's been forty thousand years of domestication. There's literally no reason to be training like this anymore.

Canine body language exists primarily to avoid conflict. Alpha theory relies on creating conflict. Conflict raises cortisol levels, leaving dogs in a heightened state of arousal, and prolonged levels of cortisol can have long-lasting negative effects on the physiological and psychological well-being of an animal (even a human), from damage to internal organs to mood disorders. Given enough stress, your dog will eventually either shut down or lash out. Sound like solid ground upon which to build a relationship? Not to me.

Force-free, also known as reward-based training, relies on finding something that your animal likes and using that to encourage them to work with you, instead of for you. This can be food, play, affection, or something completely unique to your animal and your relationship. It builds a bond based on trust and mutual respect rather than on making the dog obedient to avoid pain or punishment. Reward-based training teaches a dog what *to do*, instead of what *not to do*. It provides them cognitive stimulation and deepens your relationship because they are being guided to make choices that are then rewarded. It leads to a thinking dog who is less afraid to try new things.

There are force-free trainers who go as far as to think we shouldn't say no to our dogs, and it makes sense, because no doesn't help an animal to understand what they should do instead. It's not a cue or a behavior. So for a good long while I said to Bunny "oops" or "try again" or "no thank you" paired with requesting or demonstrating an alternative behavior. In the end, I started saying no to Bunny because I wanted her to be able to say no to me, and because often it's not about *what* is said, but *how*. I try not to use it in the context of a reprimand. I'm not perfect. It slips out, although I do my best to help her know what to do instead of telling her what not to do. Some people will say that training is about obedience, but it all feels like practice in a game of communication, and once you have effective and connective communication, then responsiveness, if not obedience, hopefully will follow.

Many trainers have now shifted from compulsion or dominance training to balanced training, which uses a combination of positive reinforcement and aversive tools including prong collars, e-collars, and leash pops. The theory employs all four quadrants of positive and negative reinforcement and punishment. I've steered clear of aversive tools, as I recognize that the fallout can be tremendous. When you see "quick-fix" trainers on social media what you are generally seeing is a dog that has been shut down. A reactive dog may indeed be dangerous, but those reactive behaviors give us information about their mental and emotional state. If we address only the behaviors through punishment without also addressing the underlying emotions, what we get is a rattlesnake without its rattle. There are many documented and researched types of fallout from using aversives, such as generalized apathy, conditioned suppression/learned helplessness, escape/avoidance, and operant aggression, but the one that seems most obvious to me is its impact on the relationship, specifically trust. I've been in human partnerships that used both psychological and physical punishment, and I can easily say that I was fearful while I was in them, felt powerless and angry, and that the best thing I ever did was to get out of them, even though I was not left unscarred and it took effort to recognize the damage that had been done.

LIMA is another subcategory on the training spectrum. It stands for: least intrusive, minimally aversive. As the name would suggest, these trainers use aversives only as a last resort if all force-free methods have proven ineffective. I consider myself a reward-based trainer. To the best of my ability I avoid punishment and rely heavily on positive reinforcement training. I'm not crazy about the labels "force free" or "purely positive" in training, if only because we are human, and just like dogs, we too can be reactive. I don't always remain cool and collected in every situation. Bunny found a chicken bone on the beach. What she saw: tasty, crunchy. What I saw: choking hazard, bone splinters, emergency vet, Bunny dies, my heart is broken, I never recover . . . dramatic, I know. I didn't have treats to trade on this day, which was a rookie mistake. Should I have had a bombproof "leave it" cue? Ideally, sure. Did I? Nope. So we'll work on that, and meanwhile I'll frantically pry it, as gently as I can, from her jaws.

Dog training is not a static science. The trainers who have been in the game the longest almost certainly have practiced methodologies that are no longer considered ethical, and the most successful dog trainers marry a wealth of experience with a willingness to grow and change as tactics and science evolve. They are able to speak to the evolution of training practices and how they actually affect our dogs. There are extreme ideologies on both ends of the spectrum.

It should be noted that force-free and positive reinforcement are not synonymous. The former is a training methodology. The latter is one of the four quadrants of operant conditioning, part of learning theory, which explains how all animals learn. By definition, positive reinforcement *always* works. The science of learning is not new. It dates back to the early 1900s, and the work of behaviorists such as Skinner, Thorndike, Pavlov, and Watson. I'll try to break it down as simply as possible.

There are two main types of conditioning, which is the process of learning by association: classical and operant. Classical conditioning is an involuntary or passive association between two stimuli. The most well-known example of this is Pavlov's dogs. He was studying salivation in dogs and noticed that they would begin to salivate when they heard his assistant's footsteps bringing them food. The salivation was an involuntary response to the stimulus (footsteps). Curious, he then paired the sound of a metronome with food delivery. At the beginning the metronome was a neutral stimulus, meaning that the dog had no learned associations with it, but after a short while the metronome by itself became a predictor of salivation, meaning that the metronome was no longer neutral and was now a conditioned stimulus. You can use classical conditioning to build positive associations with things in an animal's world that might be scary to them. For example, pairing tasty treats with the sound of a vacuum cleaner can change the association with that stimulus.

Operant conditioning (or operant learning) associates a voluntary behavior with a consequence. The learner has to actively participate and make decisions about what to do in order to receive a reward or avoid punishment. Punishment is typically used to decrease unwanted behaviors, but there are plenty of ways to do that without punishment. For example, teaching and rewarding Bunny for going to her bed when she sees our cat Ringo instead of pouncing on him positively reinforces an incompatible behavior. So the behavior of stationing becomes stronger while the behavior of pouncing becomes weaker without having to use punishment. This is where we get into the four quadrants of operant conditioning.

To simplify: Classical conditioning acts on emotions and operant conditioning acts on behavior. Both are always at play.

R+ POSITIVE REINFORCEMENT (THIS IS THE GOOD STUFF RIGHT HERE): Adding something positive to increase a behavior. Your dog chooses to sit when you say *sit*, you reward them with a treat, which strengthens that behavior in the future. I make some custom jewelry and receive monetary compensation, making it more likely that I will take on more custom orders.

R- NEGATIVE REINFORCEMENT: Removing something unpleasant to increase a behavior. In order to use negative reinforcement, something aversive has to be present so it can then be removed. Your dog doesn't sit when asked, so you push down on their bottom, yank up on their leash, or apply a shock. They sit as a result to avoid those consequences. The behavior of *sit* may be strengthened as a result, in order to avoid those actions in the future. In human terms, I brush my teeth to avoid them falling out of my head.

P+ POSITIVE PUNISHMENT: Adding something unpleasant to decrease a behavior. Your dog barks, you spray them in the face with water. They don't like that. The behavior of barking may be reduced in order to avoid being sprayed in the future. I get a ticket for going 68 in a 60 zone (even though I swear I was only going 64). I'm less likely to speed . . . maybe.

P- NEGATIVE PUNISHMENT: Removing something pleasant to decrease a behavior. Your dog pulls on the leash. Every time they do that you stop moving forward. By removing their forward movement in that moment, the pulling may decrease as the dog learns that forward motion stops when they pull. I can't go backpacking with friends because I procrastinated having that check engine light looked at and now my car says "hell no, we won't go."

Although not officially part of the four quadrants of operant conditioning, extinction is equally important when discussing behavior. Extinction is the weakening of a behavior through nonreinforcement. Nothing is added or removed from the environment. For example, a dog begs for food at the dinner table because you once gave them a tasty scrap, but you never do it again, and you ignore the begging. In theory, your dog will learn that nothing results from their puppy-dog eyes and earnest pleas, and they'll stop. Sometimes you'll see what is called an extinction burst before the behavior disappears altogether. This is marked by an increase in intensity of the reinforcement-seeking behavior just before an extinction. "It gets worse before it gets better."

Still here? This is all pretty pedantic because the quadrants can get muddy and nuanced very quickly. And while they are the "rules" of learning theory, there is so much more to it that is less definable.

And to make things more complicated, we don't get to decide what is reinforcing or punishing to our animals. What may serve as positive reinforcement for one dog may be a punisher for another. Remember the spray bottle example of positive punishment I gave? Well, I recently heard a story of a pup at day care that was repeatedly trying to incite play with dogs that were clearly not interested. This pup wasn't reading their cues despite corrections from the other dogs. The human on duty decided to intervene by spraying the pup with water. The pup immediately stopped what it was doing and came to play in the stream of water. The spray bottle was positively reinforcing. He loved it. It decreased his attention-seeking behavior from the other dogs and increased his focus on the handler. So was it both positive punishment and positive reinforcement? Oof, I don't know. There are so many contingencies. It all gets a bit confusing. I guess I generally just try to think of it in terms of: Will the action I take next hurt or scare Bunny? No? Okay. Fair game. Can we communicate effectively without fear or pain? If the answer is no, then I'm doing something wrong.

Since I had no experience training dogs before Bunny, I found myself watching a ton of training videos and just using the ones that made the most sense to me. These were videos using a whole lot of positive reinforcement. I saw videos of balanced training, too, but to me the dogs looked like they were having a whole lot less fun, and I wasn't sold on yanking a dog's leash to tell it that I'd rather it do something else when I could just show it what else to do, then give it a cookie for doing that thing. Balanced training seemed quicker, I'll give it that. Behavior modification using force-free methods can take patience, creativity, and problem-solving skills, and it is rarely linear. Both methods are effective, but I have to wonder, at what cost?

In the United States, the profession of dog training is completely unregulated. Literally anyone can call themselves a dog trainer. They can range from highly trained and accredited, including the Karen Pryor Academy (KPA CTP), Certification Council for Professional Dog Trainers (CCPDT), International Association of Animal Behavior Consultants (IAABC), Association of Animal Behavior Professionals (AABP), Certified Behavior Adjustment Training Instructor (CBATI), National Association of Dog Obedience Instructors (NADOI) . . . the list goes on. But since it's unregulated, some dog "trainers" know practically nothing about dog behavior and rely on outdated and harmful information. Fun fact: accredited organizations like these only certify positive-reinforcement-based trainers, so if your trainer isn't certified, maybe ask why. Could be they're working toward it. Could also be that they use methods not sanctioned by the American Veterinary Medical Association (AVMA) who released a statement advocating against the use of aversives following the popularity of reality television dog trainers using alpha rolls and other dominance tactics as clickbait. It is our responsibility to independently research the styles of training we want to pursue with our own furry friends. And if we plan for someone else to train them, we need to ask the important questions of those with whom we might entrust their safety. Ask about their credentials and specific methods that will be employed during training sessions. Make sure that your training philosophies align, whatever they may be.

I remember how nervous Bunny was when we first started work on skateboarding. Tail down, unsure of the strange rolling plank I was asking her to hop onto. But by letting her go at her pace and rewarding tiny steps in the right direction, she developed the confidence to skate through our living room with reckless abandon. Well, that might be an exaggeration, but she now knows that I only ask of her things I know she is capable of.

There is simply no way that Bunny and I would have come this far without a force-free philosophy. It is deeply and mutually enriching for us to overcome challenges as a team. To see the trust that she has in me, to not lead her astray, makes all the hard work worthwhile. If I am seen as "alpha," how can I use that perception to deepen trust and strengthen bonds? Hopefully through peaceful leadership, spreading a message of kindness, compassion, and communication . . . but also *ew*. Please don't call me that.

Alex the Gray

You're thinking I snuck one in here about a wizard, arncha? HA! Nope. But Alex (Avian Learning EXperiment) is unique. In some ways, he's the most likely candidate for the speaking role, and in others, the least likely. Alex is a gray parrot. I'm sure you've heard the pejorative "bird brain" before. Spoiler alert, size doesn't matter . . . brain size, geez. Thanks to the research of Dr. Irene Pepperberg, a professor and animal psychologist, we now know that bird brains are far more complex than we once thought.

Alex was one year old when Dr. Pepperberg purchased him from a pet store in June 1977. She let the sales associate pick the bird for her, careful to avoid bias at every step. She had big plans for Alex, and the thirty years she spent exploring his cognition and language capabilities resulted in one of the most well-respected examples of animal language acquisition. It was a hard-fought road, though. She was beginning her work after much of the scientific community had abandoned animal language research. She struggled to get grants. The first one she wrote came back "literally asking me what I was smoking." They had to move the research constantly, and often dealt with outright antagonism from her colleagues. Nevertheless, they persisted.

Pepperberg used a technique called *model/rival*. Most studies involving birds prior to this had used an operant paradigm. The model/rival technique is more similar to how we learn language as babies. It employs a teacher and an assistant in a social learning game wherein Alex could learn through observation how to obtain a treat. In their thirty years together, Alex learned around 150 words that he could categorize. He could count up to six and label items based on color, matter, and shape to a very high degree of accuracy. After a time, he began to teach the other parrots by participating in the model/rival with Pepperberg.

He was apparently quite sassy and would yell at the researchers if they got something wrong and slam cage doors when he was absolutely over it. He loved shredding cardboard, and once, while looking at himself in a mirror, he asked, "What color?" And so he learned the word *gray* and became the first nonhuman to ask an existential question. Bunny feels your existential dread, Alex, being the queen of it herself and the author of such classics as "dog why dog," "dog what dog is," and "who this?"

Alex passed away suddenly on September 6, 2007. His heartbreaking last words to Pepperberg as she walked out the door were, "You be good. See you tomorrow. I love you." (Feel free to take a moment here. I absolutely lost it when I first heard this.) The world and Pepperberg were devastated, but she was committed to continuing her research in the Pepperberg Lab as a part of the Alex Foundation. She and her team work with gray parrots to this day. One of them, named Griffin, has actually far exceeded the capabilities of Alex, according to Pepperberg, although for some reason he hasn't gotten much press.

Recognizing the challenges that some of her predecessors had maintaining objectivity when closely bonded with their subjects, Irene chose to view Alex as a colleague. There were all sorts of controls in place to avoid the mistakes of the past, such as blind tests and making sure that the trainers aren't the same people as the testers. Data is meticulously collected and analyzed, and the welfare of the birds is a top priority.

What I've accomplished with Bunny is not a collection of rigorously vetted data, but a series of ever-more-fascinating anecdotes. To me, that doesn't change its obvious impact. I was once fortunate enough to accidentally find myself on an interspecies IO panel during a Zoom conference. Every member is a legend (myself excluded, of course). Penny Patterson, Vint Cerf, Sue Savage-Rumbaugh, Irene Pepperberg, Paul Simon, Diana Reiss. Scientists, musicians, visionaries, pioneers, and me—yellow beanie, goofy laugh, on the verge of puking knowing that I'd have to say words in front of them all. Vint Cerf introduced me—I don't remember what I said or how long I talked for, I just remember looking around the virtual room in awe thinking, *How am I here?* In what felt like an unequivocally ballsy move, I private messaged Dr. Pepperberg during the panel to let her know how much I admired the work she'd done with Alex. Her response was something to the effect of, "Thank you. We need to be very careful." And she's right. In order to validate and bolster the credibility of the field, we need to be sure our methods are ethical and that the science is sound.

I am responsible for only one aspect of the equation: my animal companion's physical and emotional welfare, which is my passion. As I've seen in many prior animal language studies, once the analysis is done, then the focus turns to conservation and welfare. In the case of Bunny the science is secondary. I got the buttons to facilitate another avenue of communication with her, because I want to present her with every opportunity to have her needs met.

But I am glad that I can participate in and witness any shift in the direction of welfare after such collective, deep investigation, even if indirectly, of the personhood of nonhumans. Anyone who's spent a significant amount of time with an animal knows just how unique they are. That they have quirks and likes and dislikes, friends, and frenemies. That "not having grammar" feels like a funny dividing line, when at the end of the day we still play and cry together.

19

The Scientists and Bunny

I am not a speech language pathologist. I am not an animal behaviorist or dog trainer. I am not a cognitive scientist. Thankfully one doesn't need a degree to foster a deep and loving connection with another being. One simply needs to listen. But it certainly doesn't hurt to have some expert influence along the way.

On May 25, 2020, we received our first set of FluentPet prototypes from cognitive scientist Leo Trottier. Until that point, our larger Learning Resources–brand buttons had been arranged in a gridlike pattern, affixed to plywood with Velcro in no particular order. The prototypes from FluentPet were large, multicolored foam hexagons with six holes into which you'd place each button. Leo suggested I rearrange the buttons into a structure based on the Fitzgerald Key, a system developed by Edith Fitzgerald in the early 1900s to help deaf children learn grammar. This meant Bunny and I were ostensibly starting from scratch again, but that going forward Bunny would have a better chance of compartmentalizing buttons as we added words. Reorganizing made me nervous.

The first couple of days with the new system were nerve-racking. I modeled all our words in context to help familiarize her with their new locations, but she didn't seem interested in engaging with them at all. Then on the third day she started pressing WANT WHERE over and over again, which progressed to WANT WHERE MAD ALL DONE, to LOVE YOU MAD WANT WHERE ALL DONE. I was panicked at the time, but in hindsight I understand she was frustrated with the new setup and wanted to know where the old one had gone. Even those complaints were a great sign! She may have been temporarily frustrated, but she'd found a way to express that! Not long after that, it was back to business as usual.

Our board has gone through several iterations since then, the biggest of which was transitioning from the large HexTiles and buttons to the smaller version with smaller buttons. We did that in one fell swoop as well. I tried to figure out a way to transition gradually with a mixture of larger buttons and smaller buttons, but she'd favor the larger buttons when I did that, so I decided all-in was the best approach. Thankfully, since this time around we didn't change the relative positions of the individual buttons within the HexTiles, her muscle memory seemed to keep her on track, and it was a smoother shift.

Around the same time, the research study at Federico Rossano's Comparative Cognition Lab at UCSD began. While Leo worked to produce a product that helped facilitate ease of use for both human and nonhuman learners, Federico was busy designing a framework in which we could learn from and about the now thousands of animals using buttons. The goal of this study is to "use a rigorous scientific approach to determine whether, and if so, how and how much nonhumans are able to express themselves in language-like ways." There are over twenty-five hundred participants contributing data now. Mostly dogs, but also cats, horses, pigs, parrots, and even a lemur.

The study is broken into three phases:

- **PHASE 1: INITIAL DATA COLLECTION:** Participants will provide basic data regarding their learner and their learner's button usage. This will help researchers understand how age, breed, sex, teaching technique, teaching speed, and vocabulary choice affect button learning.
- **PHASE 2: VIDEO COLLECTION AND ANALYSIS:** Some participants will have cameras on their user's boards, recording continuously. That data will be sent to UCSD in order to more reliably and precisely measure the behavior and communication they produce. (We currently have six cameras on Bunny's board recording at all times. Some are sound- and motion-activated with SD cards whose data I upload every other week, and some are live streaming directly to UCSD.)
- **PHASE 3: INTERACTIVE STUDIES:** Based on insights gained in phases 1 and 2, direct and controlled tests of individual learners will be piloted. (I am not privy to exactly what these tests will look like because they don't want to bias me. These are currently happening across the United States.)

I meet weekly via Zoom with Federico and Leo to discuss what has happened during the previous week and to set observational goals for the following week. It's amazing to have their insights, and I think they appreciate mine too. After all, I approach this from the perspective of an artist.

I text them when I'm astounded or confounded, probably more than they'd like, and there have been some hilarious conversations as a result:

Leo: In this case it would suggest to us that the source of the "uncanny-ness" of the UV isn't half familiarity, but instead something else (e.g., a suppressed inclination to run a cognitive model of some "other").
Me: I understood so little of that.

Or this one:

Me: Should *am, are* go with *is, was, do, did*? Hahaa, read that out loud.

Leo: Silly. But yes, probably.

Bunny had been pressing SOUND TUG and SOUND WALK several times throughout the day for weeks. I couldn't for the life of me understand what she was trying to say. She would press these seemingly out of context. In a normal interaction with me, she'll approach the board, wait for eye contact, then begin. The same was true in these instances—approach the board, wait for eye contact, SOUND TUG. I'd pick up a tug toy that also had a squeaker in it and wave it coyly in front of her. Nothing. I'd grab a different squeaky tug and again offer it to her playfully. Again, nothing. She'd huff and walk away. Then an hour later, she'd approach the board, wait for eye contact, and press SOUND WALK. "I don't understand," I'd say. Then model with the buttons, WHAT IS SOUND WALK? More frustrated huffing. I was stumped. I brought it up with Leo and Federico, who almost instantaneously hypothesized that both phrases referred to dialogue. Tug is a back-and-forth, something that requires two participants. "Sound tug" could be a conversation. "Sound walk" is quite literally what she does when communicating with the buttons—she walks on sound. I felt dense for not having thought of it myself, but this was one of the benefits of having a team of experts to "sound walk" with. It inspired me to add TALK to her board. She began using it immediately, pressing COME TALK and BUNNY TALK and also immediately stopped using SOUND TUG and SOUND WALK.

Now the last thing I need to hear from my dog is "We need to talk," but really, who am I to stop her from saying that, if she feels the need.

It is early days in terms of the study, and while I am *so* excited to see what comes from the research, it also doesn't really matter as much to me as some may think. I don't have anything to prove. My short time together with Bunny

has been filled with surprises and laughter. Whether it's language, complex-operant conditioning, pair-associative learning, or something else entirely, it is without a doubt in my mind communication. It has absolutely strengthened our bond. Plus, presenting all this via social media means I've been able to connect with some really incredible people along the way. I'm not where I imagined I'd be at the end of 2022, but the world somehow seems full of potential and wonder more than it ever has before.

20

It's Complicated

One of the biggest challenges we faced with Bunny early on was helping her to navigate her complicated relationship with our orange tabby, Uni. He was a sweet, loud, cuddly boy who wouldn't hurt a fly. Born as a barn kitten, he came to us when he was seven weeks old. He used to spend a lot of time antagonizing our old black cat, Spooky, when she was still around, but after she was gone he mostly just slept and yelled at us for wet food. Bunny's relationship with him was one of extreme desire to play and frustration with Uni's lack of engagement. Bunny seemed to get annoyed when Uni was on Johnny's lap, although given the opportunity, she wouldn't have chosen to be there herself. Additionally, if Bunny and I were working together, whether it be tricks, obedience, or buttons, and Uni strolled casually by and I happened to notice him, her reactions could range from very concerned to humorous, as evidenced by the following interaction—which was actually rather polite given the circumstances.

Bunny was at the buttons. We were talking about poop (big surprise). I say,

"You gotta go poop right now? When poop?" Enter Uni stage right. I look at him and, anticipating potential bad blood, say, "Uni, you should head on upstairs probably." I look to Bunny and say, "Who is that, who Bunny?" Without missing a beat Bunny presses SOUND SETTLE CAT BYE, then walks around the board to sniff Uni's butt and usher him upstairs.

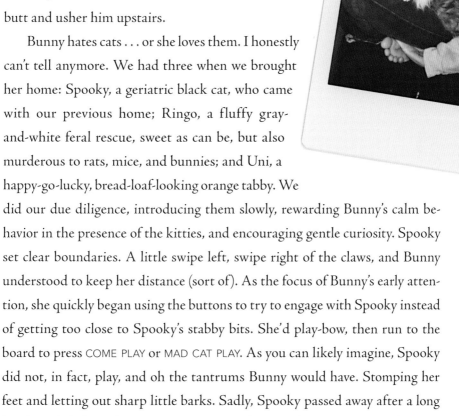

Bunny hates cats . . . or she loves them. I honestly can't tell anymore. We had three when we brought her home: Spooky, a geriatric black cat, who came with our previous home; Ringo, a fluffy gray-and-white feral rescue, sweet as can be, but also murderous to rats, mice, and bunnies; and Uni, a happy-go-lucky, bread-loaf-looking orange tabby. We did our due diligence, introducing them slowly, rewarding Bunny's calm behavior in the presence of the kitties, and encouraging gentle curiosity. Spooky set clear boundaries. A little swipe left, swipe right of the claws, and Bunny understood to keep her distance (sort of). As the focus of Bunny's early attention, she quickly began using the buttons to try to engage with Spooky instead of getting too close to Spooky's stabby bits. She'd play-bow, then run to the board to press COME PLAY or MAD CAT PLAY. As you can likely imagine, Spooky did not, in fact, play, and oh the tantrums Bunny would have. Stomping her feet and letting out sharp little barks. Sadly, Spooky passed away after a long battle with kidney disease in May 2020. The next day Bunny pressed WHERE CAT, then quickly turned her attention to Uni.

Before we brought Bunny home, I suggested to Johnny that we build some cat shelves where both Ringo and Uni could escape to, and he got right to it. A series of four platforms spiraled around a support beam in our living room, each topped with carpet for comfort and grip. Another series of platforms in the kitchen led to an elevated kitty meal station. And in our bedroom, another series of platforms against a wall led to a cat-size hanging rope bridge that worked its way up to a small loft. The cats loved them, but during the day they spent most of their time sleeping upstairs on the bed while Bunny and I worked downstairs.

Bunny makes it very clear with whom she is communicating by making direct eye contact before and after pressing buttons, and while it doesn't happen frequently, there have been several occasions recently when Bunny will press COME PLAY and I'll look up expecting that she is addressing me—but she has instead been making intense eye contact with Uni, who seems at best disinterested and at worst disgusted. In the very early days, Bunny would look at Spooky and whimper, then say CAT MAD. At times when tensions were particularly high, she'd say CAT STRANGER.

As we continued to try to foster positive vibes among the various species in our home, I was delighted to watch Bunny's verbal and nonverbal communication shift from mildly antagonistic to playful and curious, if still a bit unsure. She didn't stiffen as much when Uni came into the room. She'd approach him cautiously for a butt sniff, then stretch, look toward me for approval, and walk away. One day, after that exact, mild exchange, she walked to her board, looked at Uni, then pressed CAT FRIEND.

"Good girl!" I said. "That was so sweet!" I scratched Bunny's back, then she walked back around the board and pressed ANIMAL. And later that day, after a similar encounter with him, she pressed CAT FAMILY. Seeing the hard work we've been putting in to make her more comfortable around Uni—to shift her emotional response—being exemplified in both her actions and her words is pretty remarkable. And it reminds me that these shifts in emotional response are possible for me too. If she can do it, I can do it.

One of our neighbor's dogs found its way into our new house that summer and startled Uni, who bolted out the door and up the cliff. We searched everywhere and told all our neighbors, in addition to putting signs up, but haven't seen him since. I like to imagine that a small family of red squirrels has adopted him, and he's living a luxurious life in the treetops with them now.

Shortly after he went missing Bunny said CAT BYE.

Attention slowly shifted to Ringo, although he was around less, keeping to a much more nocturnal schedule. And while I don't think I'll ever walk in on Ringo and Bunny spooning on the couch, we'll continue to navigate complicated relationships with compassion and appropriate boundaries all the same.

We've all been there, Buns. I got you.

21

Are You Laughing With or at Me?

n Darwin's *The Descent of Man* (1872), he writes, "Dogs show what may be fairly called a sense of humor, as distinct from mere play; if a bit of stick or other such object be thrown to one, he will often carry it away for a short distance; and then squatting down with it on the ground close before him, will wait until his master comes quite close to take it away. The dog will then seize it and rush away in triumph, repeating the same maneuver, and evidently enjoying the practical joke."

Since then, research done by Patricia Simonet has shown that dogs do, in fact, produce a sound that functions effectively as a laugh. She recorded and analyzed the sounds dogs made while at play, and what she found is that in addition to the playful growls, whines, and barks, there was a sound that was similar to panting, but with more forced air, and it looked quite different from a pant when using spectrogram analysis. Simonet was encouraged by this data

to take her research further and play back some of the sounds she'd recorded to doggy participants. She noticed that individual dogs listening to the "laugh" sound would pick up toys and play-bow at the computer. In contrast, when listening to the growls, even though they were recorded during play, dogs would move away from the computer and stand by the door.

Simonet went on to design an experiment wherein she played recordings of canine laughter to shelter dogs, and after doing so, there was a significant decrease in stress-related behaviors and an increase in prosocial behaviors among them. I've tried re-creating this sound myself with Bunny, and I kid you not, when I get it right, she smiles and immediately runs over to lick my face. It may just be that she enjoys watching me embarrass myself, but we could also be sharing a laugh, and I live for that thought.

The longer I know Bunny, the more I believe that she's got a well-developed sense of humor (I mean, for a toddler). Buns likes to talk about poop, if you haven't noticed, and she'd started using it in combination with the word *play*. POOP PLAY, PLAY POOP. I hadn't thought much of it. I assumed that she was exploring buttons and chalked it up to nonsense. But it kept happening, like a lot, and I started noticing that whenever she pressed that specific combination of buttons, she'd get a huge smile on her face. You know the one, mouth open, tongue lolling, lower teeth peeking out, bright eyes.

It took me longer than it should have to figure it out. We had recently added something new to Bunny's diet, and she was GASSY! After a particularly audible event, I looked at her and said, "You farted!" I walked to the buttons and modeled MOM SMELL POOP. She immediately pressed POOP PLAY in response, then looked up at me smiling, and floppily swished her tail back and forth. "Poop play? Is that what a fart is?" I laughed. "You wanna go for a morning poop walk?" I continued. PLAY POOP, she said, smiling even more obviously than before, as if impatiently waiting for me to get the joke. "I'm pretty sure that means fart," I said, then dissolved into giggles. Bunny's stand-up bit is riddled with fart jokes, and that's fine because, quite honestly, my sense of humor hasn't evolved much past bodily functions either.

We used to get these little squeaky tennis balls for her—she loved them. She loves anything that looks like it's supposed to be a cat toy. But anyway, she'd take one of these balls, bring it right to the couch, lay down with it, then shove it as far underneath as she could with her paws, get up, run to the board, and press BALL or PLAY or HELP with a huge grin on her face. And you can't say no to that face. I mean you can, but then you're fishing seventeen tiny dust-ball-covered tennis balls out from under the couch the next day. "What is this? A joke to you?" I'd scoff. She'd answer by grabbing another ball, making direct eye contact, and shoving it under the couch. Just like Darwin's dogs with their sticks.

At this point, her humor has shifted in the way you might expect from a teenager, which means she's telling me to shut up a whole lot. SOUND SETTLE and SETTLE SOUND are terms that she has coined, which I've learned through repeated contextual usages mean "be quiet." This happens mostly during button-training sessions. As I've mentioned before, teaching Bunny words works best for us when natural learning opportunities arise, but that doesn't stop me from periodically testing to see if she'd be open to a lesson. She's not. SETTLE SOUND, she says, and walks away.

Seeing her personality come through in the things she chooses to say is an unexpected delight. At the beginning, I thought that—if we were lucky—she'd be able to request several things, like meals, water, and to go outside. That's it. Yet what I've found is so much bigger, deeper, and more layered. I'm not sure I recognize yet the impact that this could have on animal welfare and the understanding of animal cognition, but I am sure of one thing: Bunny's got *jokes*.

22

Paws Smell Like Seaweed

As a child, I spent a lot of time in my head. In my head, in the water, in the woods. These are places where I felt free. Abandoned houses, oceans, lakes, and pools, building forts alone in the forest. My imagination was my greatest escape. I was an elf or a mermaid, and I could talk to all the animals. And although I'm a bit less of a dreamer now, those physical environments still call to me on a deep level.

I lived for five years on Kauai, the majority of which was spent, you guessed it, in the water and in the jungle. I would wake up at three a.m. four days a week and drive to the end of the road at Ke'e Beach, to run along the cliffy Kalalau Trail to Hanakoa Falls. Fourteen miles round trip. I'd listen to audiobooks as I ran and wouldn't see another human for hours. I'd end my run with a swim, and then I'd begin my real-world day—but those early hours, alone and grounded, were where I felt safest and the most me.

When I moved back to Washington and met Johnny, I found similar solace alongside him. He is an accomplished rock climber and introduced me to long, multipitch climbs in the North Cascades. We were backpacking constantly and road-tripping to tackle out-of-state peaks. We summited Mount Rainier one weekend in August 2013 on a whim, and Mount Olympus that same summer. He's lived on the beach since I've known him, and I remember coming down to visit him at the beach for the first time, thinking, *Where the hell am I?* I felt like I'd been transported to a different time and place. *Magical* was the only word I could think of to describe it.

One day shortly after we'd started dating, while Johnny was out I decided to take the stand-up paddleboard out on the water. I'd paddleboarded frequently in Kauai and felt strong. I felt even stronger as I cruised down the narrows on glassy waters, fast and with zero resistance. I wasn't familiar with the tides here, but I was fairly certain that I could handle whatever this flat-watered, 75-degree day would throw at me. Little did I know that the tides here are ferocious and can reach speeds of six knots (or three meters per second), and I was currently paddling in a slack tide—a short period of time between flood and ebb currents when the water is still before switching direction. So after making my way south for about an hour, I decided to turn around and head home. I noticed that there was significantly more movement in the water, but I continued to make forward progress, albeit slowly. Fifteen minutes later, not only was I not making forward progress, I was actively moving backward, despite my best efforts. Never underestimate the power of water. It carved the Grand Canyon, for fuck's sake. I paddled across the current and into the eddy skimming the shore, and slowly made my way back to Johnny's house. It took me three hours. You'd think this would terrify me, but the thought I was left with was, *I'm never leaving.* A few years later I moved in, and we've been on the beach ever since.

One of the discussions that came up repeatedly with Johnny when we were talking about whether or not we were ready for a dog was the fact that we don't have a backyard. In fact, one of the questions that breeders and rescues will ask is, "Do you have a fenced-in yard?" We don't have a yard at all. The front of our house is tidal sea water. During low tide, we can walk the beach for miles. During high tide, we can jump from our deck into the water and swim. The diurnal winter tides here can vary from a high of +14.5 feet to a low of -3.5 feet. That's a wild swing, and although we are required to have flood insurance, there has never been a flood in the history of this community. Landslides are another story, for which there is no insurance. All the homes are connected by handcrafted boardwalks that are regularly replaced and upgraded as the sea water makes its pervasive power known. The back of our house bridges a gap to the steep slope above, which is composed of layers of clay, impervious strata, and glacial till. One of these layers has been identified by geologists as ash from the collapse of Mount Mazama, whose last eruption was in 2290 BCE, leaving behind what is now known as Crater Lake in Oregon.

This community has a rich history dating back to the early 1900s. Initially accessible only by boat, this stretch of coastline became the landing ground for tiny makeshift platforms during the summer that would house tents and small fishing cabins. After summer ended, the part-time residents would head back to their homes, and inevitably, winter storms and landslides would erase the evidence of anyone having ever been here at all. People would return the following summers and rebuild, repeating this cycle for years. Before these cabins had numbered addresses, they had names such as Rubber Inn, Bob White Camp, Sylvan Lodge, Camp Wanaton, Camp Alder, Camp Dixie, Camp Little Rock, Cliff House, Unity Club, White Caps, and Flapjack Lodge. To this day some of the modern and completely redesigned cabins retain those names as historical markers.

The first permanent resident was C. J. Ford in 1910, although strangely, he became claustrophobic (perhaps the tidal currents and tall cliffs felt oppressive to him, though to me they feel like a weighted blanket) and moved his family by boat to Alaska. Then, during Prohibition, between 1920 and 1933, the natural springs along the hillside made it a hotbed for moonshine stills. By the end of the Great Depression, most of the shacks had become year-round residences. Although damage from the frequent landslides had been mitigated some by more carefully designed construction, drunken moonshiners smoking around the stills caused several explosions that completely flattened large swaths of the community on more than one occasion. Landslides, fires, explosions. This was the pervasive pattern of life at the base of a cliff on the water. To this day we have the constant threat of landslides looming over us. Several years ago, our home narrowly escaped a huge landslide that slugged the house next to us, pinning our neighbor against a wall in her upstairs bathroom. She was fine, but moved off the beach shortly thereafter, and it took the community almost a month just to remove the mountain of clay and mud that had been deposited.

I am frequently asked why I find so much silverware and ceramics on my beach walks with Bunny, and I believe it has everything to do with this history of phoenix rising–style living. In 2001, as a result of the Nisqually earthquake, the three cabins next to our current home were taken out by a landslide. One of them was thrust completely off its pilings and floated out to sea with a tenant still inside, who had to be rescued by boat. Rumor has it that the resident, Bill, slept through the ordeal until the boat puttered up to save him. Living here does not come without its challenges, but I wouldn't have it any other way.

Several times, because of these threats, the city of Tacoma tried to have the community completely torn down—but in the 1970s, and after long debate among politicians, the city's official stand moved from one of removal to one of preservation. The Shoreline Management Act prohibited new overwater construction, thus halting the growth of the community, while also protecting it on the National Register of Historic Places.

The community is well-seated now, and there are even tour boats that putter by daily in the summer, announcing over megaphone the history of this special place, pointing out the beehives where moonshine stills used to be, the life-size bronze mermaid that sits atop a boulder mid-beach, and taking note of the unique characteristics that each cabin possesses. Sometimes we wave as they pass, sometimes neighbors gather on decks to collectively about-face and moon the passengers and crew. That's just how we roll down here.

I learned a huge portion of the narrative of our community from our resident historian and neighbor Roger, who, when I first started coming down to the beach as Johnny's guest, told another neighbor, "I just don't trust redheads." Now when I see him he says, "I'm putting you in charge of the beach doggy directory." He himself prints the neighborhood directory of beach homes, residents, phone numbers, and email addresses biannually, and personally walks them door to door. I suppose he thinks that because I have a particular affinity for dogs now that I ought to feel compelled to do the same for the rather large collection of canines down here. Does he think they'll be calling each other? Setting up their own playdates? Unclear. I never know if he's joking or not so I just say, "On it!" with an awkward giggle, then continue on my way.

Moving to, on, or off the beach presents special challenges because there is no road access between homes, just the narrow boardwalks barely wide enough for one person, so any large items need to be moved in or out by boat or barge, timed carefully with the high tides. For this reason, when we made a move in 2015, it was lateral—from one cabin to the next. This is the case for many long-time residents, and sometimes conversation will lead to, "Well, when I lived in your house . . ." and the stories are as sordid and silly as you might expect. One of my neighbors lived in our previous home long before I was born. Another, who has since moved off the beach, set off fireworks inside every Fourth of July. I don't have much context for that story, but somehow it didn't surprise me. Many of the homes have seen people in their final days, and most of them have been witness to a child's entrance into the world. They all have

stories to tell, and I feel privileged to be a part of the community.

As it so happens, we moved laterally once again in June 2021. So much of a move down here is about timing, luck, and word of mouth. The selling and purchasing agent for 99 percent of the homes is a neighbor of ours, and the previous occupant of the home was Selena and her family. A veritable musical chairs of home ownership and rental. We'd been dreaming of more space. A studio with room for me to breathe and be inspired in, an office for Johnny to invent in and to create engaging lessons and labs for his kids (he teaches high school physics and engineering). We wanted a home where our 500-pound laser cutter wouldn't take up the majority of the living room, and a space where, if we decided to add another dog to our family, we'd have plenty of room for cats, dogs, and humans to happily coexist.

I started filling 150-pound contractor bags with trash or donation items a month before the move. It was a long overdue process. It's amazing how much one can accumulate thoughtlessly over the years, and it felt freeing to let so much of it go. We offered pieces of furniture that we no longer wanted to community members who'd come by with a hand truck or boat to scoop them up. Everyone we passed on the trail was curious and congratulatory, and many offered their boat or hands to help. It's a grueling process though, and if we were able to do it ourselves, we preferred the hard labor and subsequent reward. "Type-2 fun," as our climbing buddies like to refer to it. A real suffer-fest.

At any rate, the day we got the keys, the real moving began. The tides weren't ideal. The highs weren't very high, and they were taking place during suboptimal hours—5:00 a.m. and 8:00 p.m. We made three boatloads that first night, moved everything inside and went back to our old house to sleep, setting an alarm for 4:30 a.m. Every day for the next week and a half we made upwards of four boat trips a day and multiple wagonloads back and forth along the quarter-mile boardwalk between homes, Bunny accompanying us back and forth. She was using her board less during this time, mostly because we weren't around it much, but the brief moments that we were, she'd press a quick UGH or CONCERNED, leaving me worried about how she would adjust to the move.

On the third day we moved our mattress and our couch, carefully rigging them to the hoist on our davit—a small cranelike device used to lift and lower things. We lowered them down onto the motorized sardine can that we call a boat. It was slack tide and there was no wind, so we crossed our fingers and hoped for the best. Success! Although there was a davit at our new home, there was no hoist, so we were beaching the boat, then carrying all our belongings up the beach and onto the deck. Not ideal. Our new home came with a tool shed replete with piles of decades-old tools and cobweb-covered building materials. During low tide on the third day, we decided to clear it out to make space for our gear. Lo and behold, at the bottom of one of the piles, a hoist! Rusted? Yes. In working condition? Turns out, also yes! Johnny affixed the hoist to the davit and moving got a tiny bit easier from there on out . . . until the hoist at our old place stopped working. Beach problems, amirite?

I brought Bunny's board over that night, and the next morning she said her first words in our new home. Johnny was lying on the couch. I said to Bunny,

"We family. We home." She looked at me, walked over to Johnny and licked his face, walked to the window as if to survey her new surroundings, and then to the board to press MOM, YES.

Moving was by no means over once all our belongings were in our new home. We still had twenty-odd contractor bags full of trash or donations and a couple of pieces of furniture that Johnny would need to boat around the peninsular point, where I'd meet him with the truck to unload and run to the dump. It was an arduous process, but every day our house felt more and more like home, and Bunny really seemed to love it. We took Ringo and Uni to our new home by canoe, believing that it would be a less stressful ride than by motorboat. I'm not convinced that there is a zero-stress way to move cats, but we did the best we could, and they, too, seemed to be finding their rhythm.

Having settled comfortably into a life that revolves around physical environs that soothe the nervous system, we make a point to walk the beach every day when the tides allow. Bunny searches for olfactory treasures, I look for agates and petrified wood and frequently find silverware and pottery shards in homage to the complex history of this place. Then to the woods we'll head, letting Bunny set the pace and choose our path, lost in thought and free.

Chaser, the World's Smartest Dog (feat. Rico)

When I started getting into the history of animal language studies, I was expecting way more dog stories. If we wanted to communicate with animals, why not start with the creature we'd spent thousands of years coevolving with? We literally gave dogs the title "man's best friend," but we've got scientists running around trying to talk to dolphins and gorillas? I'm just saying, it seemed sus. Trying to get to the bottom of this led me to Chaser and Rico, the Border collies. Both dogs developed extraordinary receptive language capability. Rico knew the names of around two hundred fifty toys and could pick one out by name from a pile of hundreds. Not only that, but he could infer a new toy's name on the first try through deductive reasoning and still remember it a month later—a process known as fast-mapping.

Chaser, deemed the world's smartest dog, also had an astounding receptive vocabulary. She knew more than a thousand proper nouns and was similarly adept at fast-mapping. She had the largest tested vocabulary of any nonhuman in the world and was proven to be able to comprehend sentences containing a prepositional object, verb, and direct object (syntax). She knew modifiers like bigger, smaller, faster, and slower. Chaser's human could say something like "to ball take Frisbee" and Chaser would find the ball, then take it to the Frisbee and drop it. And she understood that when the order of the words was changed, it meant a different thing. Chaser's proven understanding of these three elements of grammar demonstrated a huge leap in what was previously thought cognitively possible by canines.

Her guardian and trainer, Dr. John W. Pilley, was a professor emeritus at Wofford College and wanted to test the established boundaries of canine cognition. So when, at the age of seventy-four, he received a Border collie pup from his wife on Christmas Day, he set to work, making this the coolest retirement story I've heard. Like, okay, I'm done with my brilliant teaching career so now, mmm, I dunno, perhaps I'll change the course of history by teaching my dog a gajillion words. Yeah, that sounds about right. Lol.

Anyway, I was super inspired by their story and their relationship. I read Dr. Pilley's book about their journey and was greatly saddened when I learned that he had passed away in 2018. I've often thought about him and wondered what he might think of the work we are doing.

On the morning of September 27, 2020, I found an email in my in-box with the subject heading "Bunny and Chaser" from Dr. Pilley's daughter, Deb Pilley Bianchi. She was Chaser's cotrainer, and is the founder of the Chaser

Initiative, which is dedicated to educating children K–12 about the power of play. She had come across a post I'd made, talking about my admiration for the work of Dr. Pilley, and had been moved. We scheduled a Zoom call for the next day.

Now I know this sounds cheesy, but from the moment I got on that call with Pilley, I felt a connection to her. We talked about Bunny, and my journey with her, and about Chaser and her quirks. I shared my sadness that her father was not around to witness the work so many people—researchers and animal guardians alike—were now doing to better understand their dogs. We talked about the importance of connection and of building a solid foundation for communication by taking the time to understand our animals *on their terms* first. It is a gift that they choose to communicate with us in this way. It is a show of trust and engagement built through the hard work of a partnered dynamic. After all, dogs are telling us things all the time, and the onus is first and foremost on us to help them feel heard.

She and I both shed tears as we talked. She told me that her father would be so proud. In that moment, I realized why I'd felt sadness when reading about the language studies with primates: apes have not spent the last twenty thousand years or so coexisting with humans, evolving to work and play with us, sleep and eat with us, empathize with and annoy us. Dogs have. There is something that feels so selfish about removing a wild animal from its natural habitat so that we can learn more about us. It's not like the other animal language studies were necessarily abusive—although some of them certainly had questionable ethics, and many of them unhappy endings—but with dogs it somehow feels like a natural next step in cooperation. Many of us already feel like we can read our dog's minds and vice versa, and I continue to be hopeful that, as with our journey, this process inspires others to really meet their dogs in the middle by learning how they communicate naturally. Give it a chance—it's incredible to watch.

23

Friends Are the New Poop

When Bunny was about one, we added buttons for the names of her three best dog friends. They each lived within a five-minute walk of our house, which made it easy to reinforce her requests, provided the pups were available after a quick text to their humans. I'm deeply introverted. I form strong attachments to a very small group of people, and I think Bunny is the same way. She is naturally quite attached to Johnny and me but has, over the last few years, also formed sweet attachments to a few neighborhood dogs whom she now requests by name.

Tango, a young wirehaired pointing griffon; Selena, a standard poodle just a couple of months older than Bunny; and Beacher, a golden Lab and the baby of the group. I conditioned their names by making sure that when she was playing with each of those friends, I said their names repeatedly—"Tango

friend, Bunny play Tango now"—and when we'd come home, I'd model ALL DONE PLAY TANGO. BUNNY DID PLAY TANGO.

Our mornings were full of friend requests. WHERE TANGO, FRIEND BEACHER, GO SELENA, and this interaction:

Bunny: *See love you Selena*

Me: You love Selena? We did play Selena morning.

Thinking circle (*She regularly does this between thoughts. She'll walk a circle around a table, the buttons, a chair.*)

Bunny: *Beacher*

Me: Beacher is friend. We did play Beacher yesterday.

Bunny walks to the window to look for Beacher, who lives next door.

Me: That's where Beacher lives. See Beacher home.

Bunny: *Tango*

Me: We're going to see Tango soon. We go play Tango soon.

She knew exactly where each of these friends lived and would run to their respective doors and wait in a wiggly, seated position until they came out. It was really cute.

She's always been most successful with one-on-one play, as I think most dogs are. I can relate, and although I don't spend as much time as I'd like with my friends these days, it's nice to imagine that she thinks about hers as fondly as I do mine.

Bunny is sensitive to social pressure and to the way new dogs approach her. I wonder sometimes if perhaps she isn't socialized as well as she could be

(I wonder that about myself, too, if I'm being honest), but I think I did everything I was supposed to. I exposed her from a young age to many different types of environments, people, places, things, and other dogs. I tried to ensure that those experiences were strongly positive, and they were. The pandemic changed the way all of us socialize, not that we'd had many guests in our home before it, but we certainly didn't have any during it.

A dog's reaction to a nonverbal communication from another dog can take a split second, and unless we know exactly what to look for it can be challenging to mitigate or avoid negative interactions without just keeping distance, which is sometimes unavoidable. We can't always control what other dogs do, but what I've found works well for Bunny when facing a new dog is a three-second introduction. Just a quick sniff, then walk away. If they are still interested, we'll do another three-second sniff greeting. Usually at this point Bunny will shake off and relax a bit. At that point, I'll add a bit of levity.

Additionally, I find that my emotional state can directly impact hers during these encounters. The sillier I am, the more likely she is to relax and adopt a playful demeanor too. Sometimes it's best just to walk away, but I've been able to turn interactions into positive spaces just by becoming more playful myself. Our dogs really do look to us for guidance. I've only ever worked with Bunny, so I don't know how this may or may not work for other dogs, but I definitely notice a parallel in human communication. I frequently use humor to disarm, disengage, or distract in uncomfortable situations. It is a very real coping mechanism. I am not afraid to appear ridiculous, and I believe it is a powerful tool in opening lines of communication.

24

And That's on Curiosity

Part of my journey with Bunny has involved research into AAC, augmentative and alternative communication, and what conditions and diagnoses necessitate its use. First, though, let's talk more specifically about what AAC is.

AAC is everywhere. Every time you point, write, wave, or smile, you are using AAC. There are two main categories: aided and unaided. Unaided uses natural methods of bodily communication such as facial expressions, gestures, and signing. Aided systems range from very basic to very high tech. An example of basic aided AAC would be writing, pressing a button, or pointing to letters, pictures, or words on a board. Higher-tech models include speech-generating devices in tablet form. They allow for efficient and effective communication, while also providing alternate methods of word, phrase, and letter selection, such as eye tracking and head tilting.

Department of Applied Mathematics and Theoretical Physics
Silver Street, Cambridge, England CB3 9EW

Telephone: Cambridge (0223) 337900
Telex: 81240 CAMSPL G FAX 33 7918

S W Hawking, C B E, F R S
Lucasian Professor of Mathematics

8th June 1989

Alexis Rose Kane,

Dear Alexis,

Thank you for writing to Professor Hawking. I am sorry that Stephen can not reply to your letter himself, but I will try to answer your questions.

First of all, if all the planets in the universe disappeared, the universe would be just the same, except that there wouldn't be any planets. This would mean that we would not exist, because you need a special planet (like the earth) with just the right temperature and air and water and so on, for life like us to grow.

Things would be a bit different if all the matter in the universe disappeared. That is, if all the planets, stars, black holes and clouds of gas disappeared. Then the universe would either not exist at all, or it would be empty space stretching out to infinity in all directions. Again, we would not exist. In fact nobody could see a universe like this, because if there was somebody to see the empty universe, it would not be empty any more. The only way we can know what it might be like, is by using mathematics.

A black hole is a region of space from which light can not escape. A black hole can be formed when a large star collapses until it is just a few miles across. It has to be a very big star, at least twice as big as our sun. A star collapses at the end of its life when it has burnt nearly all the fuel it needs to keep shining. Things are pulled into a black hole by the force of gravity. This is the same force that makes things fall towards the Earth. In fact all matter pulls other matter towards it by gravity. The heavier something is, the more it pulls. Something as big and heavy as the Earth pulls enough that you can easily see it by dropping a stone. But a black hole is much, much heavier than the Earth. With a black hole, the pull of gravity is so strong that nothing can escape once it has fallen in. Nothing can travel faster than the speed of light, and even light can not get out of a black hole (this is why they are called 'black' holes).

I am not sure that scientists are totally agreed about how planets form. However, the only theory that I have heard is this: The solar system is formed by a large cloud of gas and dust (mostly hydrogen gas) which gradually collapses due to gravity and heats up. Most of the gas ends up as the fuel for the sun. But some of the gas and dust sticks together to form the planets and moons in the solar system. At first the planets are very hot too. But after a long time the outside surface of the planet cools down and forms rocks. The centre of the Earth, is still very hot and is made from molten rock. This can be seen when a volcano erupts.

I hope that my answers are good enough for you.

I am age 23 and like music, science and flying.

Yours sincerely

Andrew M. Dunn (Graduate Assistant)
On behalf of Professor S. W. Hawking

Some of the conditions that could bring about a need for an AAC include life (just throwing this one out there as a reminder that literally everyone uses AAC in one form or another), Alzheimer's, Parkinson's, stroke, cerebral palsy, traumatic brain injury, learning disabilities, autism spectrum disorder, and ALS. Perhaps the most well-known AAC user was Stephen Hawking, the theoretical physicist who suffered from ALS and used a computer to communicate verbally, but all of the AAC users I've spoken to during my time with Bunny have been autistic.

There are an estimated five million people in the United States who cannot rely on speech to be understood, and well over two million of them are using AAC. An estimated 25 to 30 percent of autistic people will never develop verbal speech. Some will need AAC to communicate all the time, and some may only need it intermittently. Whatever their support needs are, AAC users deserve to be heard. Communication is a right, not a privilege, for all living beings.

My first encounter with someone who used AAC was, in fact, Stephen Hawking. When I was ten, I wrote him a letter. I had become obsessed with and frightened by the immense power of black holes and decided that the only way to allay my fears was to speak with the preeminent expert. I remember asking my mum, "How will he write back?" I don't remember her response. I thought I'd won the lottery when I received a letter in return from the University of Cambridge, Department of Applied Mathematics and Theoretical Physics. Professor Hawking himself had not responded, but his gracious graduate assistant Andrew M. Dunn (who helped Hawking to revise his book *A Brief History of Time*) had. I don't remember what I wrote in my letter to him, but in classic ten-year-old pen pal fashion, I must have signed off with something like "I am ten, I like art and ponies and writing letters," because Andrew ended his letter with, "I am age 23 and like music, science, and flying. Yours sincerely, Andrew."

This experience was part of a deepening understanding for me about the value and power of communication, although I didn't realize it at the time.

When it comes to communication with Bunny, I'm more concerned with honoring her as a dog than increasing her ability to communicate like a human. The beauty of our relationships with animals is that we have the potential to "get" each other in spite of the language barrier. That to me seems more miraculous than a dog telling me they want to play "tug" in my words. But this is what motivated me to pursue buttons in the first place. We were going to "get" each other. I was going to make sure of that.

The power of the buttons has not been so much that it gave Bunny words, but that it inspired me to dig deeper. To follow with creativity a benevolent curiosity centered in a galaxy of sciences that I knew nothing about, and see what happened. At the end of the day, the more opportunities we take to examine experiences outside our own, the broader our perspective becomes. And with that, an understanding of the nuance and beauty within communication.

25

The Shoe Fit

I don't know if this is really going to come as much of a surprise to anyone, it certainly didn't to me, but getting an official diagnosis was a somewhat unexpected side quest during this journey with Bunny. I'm autistic.

I have a propensity for diving deep into special areas of interest, at times to the exclusion of most everything else. I'll research a thing until I feel like it was born in my brain. These special interests have primarily been art related—painting and collage, street art, jewelry and wearable art design, dance, even the art of pairing sake with the perfect cheese in what might be the most unusual crossover ever. And now, of course, there's Bunny. Communication is the most enigmatic and sublime art form of them all. My interest in this is made all the more fascinating by the fact that one of the diagnostic criteria for autism includes challenges in social communication.

In a lot of ways, I owe my successes to single-mindedness, but I've also found it to be alienating. It can be difficult for me to maintain relationships when I am completely consumed for weeks, months, or even years by one thing.

I find it hard to relate to people who don't share my particular interests, or who aren't as excited to hear about them as I may be to talk about them, in which case I may find it difficult to talk about anything at all. Social situations without the aid of alcohol have always been a struggle, and now sober, I find the practice of small talk to be just that: a practice. I've had to learn the "art" of talking about nothing, but it always leaves me feeling insincere and exhausted.

The ins and outs of social nuance are mysterious, and perhaps this is why it has felt particularly simple to connect with Bunny. We may not always under-stand each other, but she doesn't ever "say" one thing and mean another. There are fewer layers that I have to peel back to get to the point. It's comforting, this sort of relationship. And now that I've found it, I wonder how my life may have been different if I'd found it sooner.

I learned more about myself in the first year with Bunny than I had in all my previous forty. Something about the examination of how we know another being, so different from and yet so similar to ourselves, that allowed me to peer objectively at my own life's experiences with more compassion. And this is wild because it's something that twenty-plus therapists, three long stays in the hospital, meditation, medication, journaling, and even a shamanic exorcism (I'll literally try anything once) couldn't seem to accomplish.

Autism is a neurological condition as opposed to one that is solely psycho-logical or behavioral. The physiology of an autistic brain processes sensory in-put in a completely unique way. Autistic people are born autistic, but the reason for so much recent late diagnosis is that we now know that although symptoms must be present in early childhood, they may not be fully manifest until so-cial or sensory demand exceeds capacity. Plus these symptoms are frequently exhaustively masked or hidden from public view in an attempt to adhere to social norms, which means that not all autism fits into our obvious stereotypes. And although the diagnostic criteria for autistic men and women is the same, their symptoms can present quite differently. Autism and intellectual disability were at one point categorized as one disorder, which is likely responsible for many of the existing stereotypes. They are separate, but not infrequent, comorbidities.

I'd certainly had thoughts growing up that Asperger's syndrome may have been a relevant diagnosis for me. But at a certain point, I stopped hearing the term Asperger's and it all but disappeared from my vocabulary. Turns out, the diagnosis of Asperger's was removed from use by the American Psychological Association in 2013 and replaced by the broader Autism Spectrum Disorder (ASD). The World Health Organization followed suit in 2019. And why was it removed from use? Well, because initially Asperger's syndrome was added to the diagnostic manual in order to refine treatment and assessment, but the results were variable and the general consensus among researchers was that Asperger's and autism were more alike than they were different.

Oh, and also, Hans Asperger is thought to have been a Nazi eugenicist. Although he never actually joined the Nazi Party, he worked directly for them and was responsible for signing papers that sent several children to their deaths. Asperger's diagnostic predecessor was "autism psychopathy." Under Hitler's regime, psychiatry turned from a practice of compassion to one of weeding out those perceived to be "genetically inferior." Doctors were required to report disabled children in their care, and those who were deemed intelligent or useful were kept alive and the rest were sent to child euthanasia centers, where their deaths were recorded as pneumonia and other ailments.

Despite this revolting ideology, Hans Asperger did have some markedly forward things to say: "It seems that for success in science and art, a dash of autism is essential . . . the necessary ingredient may be an ability to turn away from the everyday world, from the simply practical, an ability to rethink a subject with originality so as to create in new untrodden ways." And I can't say I disagree. Autism is not a new phenomenon, and there are people in history whom we can look back upon with our new understanding and postulate that they might have been experiencing this unique neurological state. In some more recent cases, we know of actual diagnoses, such as Temple Grandin and Sir Anthony Hopkins. And some of the recorded behaviors and experiences of the deeply creative and inventive Nikola Tesla or eighteenth-century clockmaker John Harrison or Hans Christian Andersen make it tempting to diagnose them posthumously. The fact is that many creators in history who we might call geniuses leave evidence that they were likely neurodivergent in some way.

I was officially diagnosed with autism spectrum disorder in 2020, after many months of deeply relating to articles I read about autistic women and learning as much as I could about neurodiversity. I went on to learn about masking, stimming, dysregulation, and sensory overload, which unlocked poignant reminders of struggles I'd had since childhood. It was as if I hadn't had the language to describe my experiences up until this point. It was simultaneously revelatory and overwhelming. The structure of my life had changed so much over the last year, making space for a thousand new ways of feeling and experiencing the world. Is it possible to feel lost and found at the same time? I think so, because I did.

I made an appointment—well, several appointments—for neuropsych evaluations with a registered psychotherapist. I'd seen countless therapists over the years, yet none had suspected it. How? I'd received diagnoses of generalized anxiety disorder, depression, OCD, alexithymia, trauma, and PTSD. Some of them stuck, but no amount of talk therapy really seemed to get to the core of my experience. I took a litany of tests, answered hundreds of questions, and began to reevaluate a life's worth of experiences through a new lens. I struggled to process how I was feeling about all this new information. Was it sorrow? Could it be relief? Perhaps anger?

The answer turned out to be yes. I was saddened that for so much of my life I'd felt like an alien, never quite understanding how to function socially. I learned how to mask characteristics and behaviors that weren't "normal." I became a chameleon. I *could* fit in everywhere, but at great cost. When you become too good at blending in, you lose all sense of who you actually are. And as it turns out, I wasn't doing that great a job at it anyway. I felt relief at the fact that I finally had an answer, one that resonated more deeply than anything had before, and I was angry that I had gone undiagnosed for so long.

For as long as I can remember, I've studied humans in the wild, carefully observing the social standard. Taking mental notes on what works and what doesn't within certain circles. "Why are you staring?" they'd ask. I quickly learned to be more covert. In group settings, I am initially quiet until I can read the room and determine who I need to be. Many of my interactions are scripted. I've adopted the mannerisms, speech patterns, and fashion of people I wanted to seem like. I'd laugh at jokes I didn't understand, and nod in agreement, saying, "Yeah totally," even when I wasn't processing the words at all. In places where many sounds and conversations converge, it takes extraordinary effort to filter just one out, and more often than not, I simply have to remove myself to a quieter place. I scored remarkably high on my IQ test and yet have always felt slow.

I learned to hide physical mannerisms that seem out of place in a neurotypical world, such as rocking back and forth on my feet, or vocal stims like repeating a word or phrase for days or humming the same song to the beat of my steps when I walk. A stim is a self-regulatory mechanism for coping with either overstimulation or lack of stimulation. They are repetitive movements or sounds and are part of the diagnostic criteria for autism. Everyone stims, both allistic (nonautistic) and autistic. A tapping foot, nail biting, hair twirling—these are not exclusive to autists, but in some cases stims can become dangerous or socially isolating, which leads to deeper masking, which eventually leads to

burnout. For the last several years, my primary stim and special interest had been chain mail. Opening and closing rings, finding and creating patterns, turning those patterns into wearable art that felt akin to a weighted blanket for my soul. I would literally spend twelve hours a day completely focused, in a rhythm, building link by link, angry when I inevitably had to stop in order to sleep.

Before that it was origami. Everywhere I'd go, I'd leave a paper trail of frogs, flowers, elephants, boxes, cranes. Mostly cranes. I was inspired by the story of Sadako Sasaki, who lived through the bombing of Hiroshima, but subsequently fell ill from cancer as a result of nuclear fallout. Japanese folklore says that a crane can live for a thousand years, and a person who folds a thousand origami cranes will have their wish granted. Upon hearing this story, Sadako began folding. Sadly, she passed away after folding thirteen hundred cranes and a long battle with leukemia, but her legacy has inspired hope and spreads a message of peace to this day. Three times in my life I have intentionally folded one thousand paper cranes, the most recent of which is when I was hospitalized for a month for an out-of-control eating disorder and drug and alcohol addiction at the age of twenty-eight. The practice became a meditation for me, and although I am not necessarily a believer in granted wishes, I was fairly certain that my eating disorder would kill me, and this repetitive folding brought me comfort.

When I was living in Kauai, I adopted a habit of wagging like a dog when I was happy, just a joyous little rump shake accompanied by me saying "wag wag wag" under my breath. It felt good. It didn't cross my mind that it might seem weird to casual observers. One day at work, at a bar in Hanalei, I was waiting, gently wagging, for the bartender to make a cocktail for one of my customers, and a stranger sitting there, drink in hand, asked the bartender what I was doing, to which she replied, "I dunno, she's wagging or something." The customer looked at me and said "weird." They laughed. I never did it again.

I've learned that autism in women is far more likely to go undiagnosed, in large part due to our amazing yet self-injurious ability to internalize, adapt, and camouflage. We all do this to some extent. Our Western culture demands it of us when we enter spaces and interactions designed for men, but for me it led to decades of being completely shut down, not having any idea who I was, and adopting many harmful coping mechanisms out of sheer subconscious desperation.

I wish I'd known sooner, but I'm thankful that I know now. Without Bunny's influence, I may never have come to this diagnosis. As she unwittingly led the way, it became a notion that my consciousness could no longer ignore, despite my best efforts. And as I opened myself to the possibility, elements of my history came into focus, allowing for a more compassionate path to my future.

Alexandre Rossi

The first studies about dogs using lexigrams and buttons were done in the early 2000s, but anecdotal successes seem to go as far back as the 1970s. Until recently, most language studies done with dogs had been focused on comprehension or receptive language and not on production or expressive language.

Enter Brazilian animal behaviorist Alexandre Rossi. Inspired by the tests run with Kanzi the bonobo, Rossi became the first person to use buttons with recorded words with a dog in this manner. To help him with this research, Rossi recruited his own dog, Sofia, whom he had rescued from the streets as a small puppy.

Rossi gave Sofia buttons that would play an audio command when pressed. The buttons Rossi provided to Sofia were: *walk, crate, water, food, toy, petting,* and *urine*. Sofia was kept in his home as a pet, and special attention was paid to her well-being and motivation to communicate. Sofia wasn't required to press any buttons in order to have her needs met. She was able to generalize *toy* to a variety of play objects, and *food* to a variety of food items (including a guinea pig she once met). Reminds me of the time Bunny said BIRD GO BELLY while observing a sea gull just outside the window.

The published, peer-reviewed paper resulting from this study was incredible to read. So many of the patterns they documented and training techniques they had employed were similar to what I'd used in the first six months of my time with Bunny. It was interesting to compare techniques employed by Rossi and Christina Hunger (the only two people I knew who had done work like this with dogs). The study also addressed the Clever Hans effect and provided nearly irrefutable evidence to undermine an interpretation of the Rossi/Ades experiment as such.

From the abstract of the 2007 study, "A Dog at the Keyboard: Using Arbitrary Signs to Communicate Requests," by Alexandre Pongrácz Rossi and César Ades: "A female mongrel dog was submitted to a training schedule in which, after basic command training and after acquiring the verbal labels of rewarding objects or activities, she learned to ask for such objects or activities by selecting lexigrams and pressing keys on a keyboard. Systematic records taken during spontaneous interaction with one of the experimenters showed that lexigrams were used in an appropriate, intentional way, in accordance with the immediate motivational context. The dog only utilized the keyboard in the experimenter's presence and gazed to him more frequently after key pressing than before, an indication that lexigram use did have communicative content."

What I love about Rossi's research with Sofia, of course, is how their relationship played an invaluable role in their success. Had Sofia not enjoyed the process, they would have stopped, and she would've continued her life as Rossi's beloved companion. And that's just what happened after they completed the study. It's an element of ethical stability that I missed in the ape studies, which seems to involve asking "Can I?" but not "Should I?"

26

Kona and Kauai

When I was thirty, I moved back to Seattle after having spent five years in Kauai. Living there had been challenging and transitional—beautiful and grotesque. Like many times in my life, a persistent "go big or go home" mentality meant that I was all in, wherever I was, whatever I was doing. Kauai had been that.

One thing I love about Kauai is its conspicuous lack of dangerous land critters (for a tropical environment). There are no crocodiles or bears, mountain lions or snakes. And only a couple of venomous insects including the Black Widow spider and the giant centipede. Now the latter isn't technically an insect but rather an arthropod named Scolopendra. I say that out loud in the voice of Lord Voldemort from the Harry Potter series. I can't seem to say it any other way, and while I'm not particularly afraid of most creepy crawlers, these buggers legitimately frighten me. They're brownish red with orange legs, the front

two of which are modified to act as poison-filled fangs, and they can get up to ten inches long. I rarely saw them aside from the occasional overturned rock or log on a jungle run, and I was glad of that. All of the longtime residents had stories about having been bitten and the ensuing emergency room visits and excruciating pain. So, imagine my delight when I was awakened one morning at three a.m. by a light tickle on my neck. In the dark, I raised my hand to the spot and felt movement. Instinctively I grabbed around, and my fingers found purchase. As I drew my hand away from my neck, I could feel each and every leg of a giant centipede losing its grip one by one, like a zipper. Good news: It was off my neck. Bad news: It was writhing in my hand and had whipped around to bite me at the base of my thumb. Reflexively I threw it across the room and ran to turn on the lights. By the time they were on, the centipede had disappeared and I could see my heartbeat in my thumb. The flesh around the puncture wounds was immediately hot and swollen and sweating. I ran to the bathroom to take some aspirin and run the wound under hot water to reduce the swelling and dilute the venom. It was only then that I noticed my neck. Hoping to turn me into one of its own, apparently, it had bitten me in the middle of the right side of my neck; it too was swollen and sweating. Surprisingly, it didn't hurt as much as I'd imagined. I considered going to the emergency room, but in the end, I just went back to bed with the lights on. Eight hours later, I was fine but I did have what looked like a vampire bite on my neck for about a month.

I'd moved to Kauai, in large part to escape a pattern of behavior that I intrinsically understood would eventually lead to self-destruction, but also for a guy. We didn't last, but we stayed together for a couple of years. He had a dog named Cooper, an enormous Labrador–pit bull mix. He was very sweet to me, but aggressive toward other dogs. I guess this was my first experience with a reactive dog, but that word wasn't even on my radar. I rarely walked him because it was scary to do so, and I was in a pretty dark place to begin with.

The toxic coping mechanisms that I'd hoped to abandon by leaving Seattle followed me with renewed fervor, excited to inflict their punishments in novel territory. Yes, I was running away from my problems, and no, it didn't work. Those problems still existed, I just had fewer friends, albeit fewer toxic friends, and better beaches. What felt initially like it could've been a fresh start, a new me, was in fact the same me in a new place. I should've known. Perhaps this sounds like I'm being unnecessarily hard on myself, but I really should have known. I could feel myself losing my grip on control after only a few months, and by the end of the first year I was careening recklessly toward another two-month-long stay in the hospital. That's the thing about control. I only feel safe when I have it, but my focus becomes so narrow trying to get it that I practically cease to exist.

I learned a great deal while I was on Kauai, and after my stay in the hospital, things got a bit better for me. I cultivated an extraordinary love for trail running and for being alone with my thoughts. I've never been a lonely person, always comfortable for days without seeing or speaking to another soul. I was regularly called a "lone wolf" by bosses who wanted me to participate more in group activities or chastised by friends who thought I wasn't making an effort to connect. I couldn't imagine a more beautiful place to spend so much time alone. There were empty beaches where I could swim and free dive for shells, miles of trails in canyons and jungles to explore, but at a certain point even those began to feel oppressive. The island was small. I was bored, and boredom is dangerous for me. I needed a bigger space to explore, both physically and emotionally, so I moved back to Seattle.

The move was simple. I sold all my belongings, packed a bag with my clothes, most of which wouldn't be useful in the colder Pacific Northwest climate, and hopped on a plane. I moved in with one of the few friends that has remained constant in my life, Tanya, and immediately began looking for a job in food service. I interviewed at a couple of places that didn't feel quite right, then finally accepted a job at a trendy Mexican-fusion chain where all the servers were super hip and pretty. I'd been training there for a week or so when the owner came in to meet the new employees and speak with management, making the rounds from store to store. He observed my shift, and when I was done he came over and said, "Good work today, but you'd look a lot cuter if you smiled more." I never went back.

Instead, I accepted a position at a new, high-end Japanese restaurant near Lake Union. The owner, Steve, was amazing, and the other employees seemed great. I had a solid knowledge base already from having worked in Japanese fine dining while on Kauai. It was at this job that I made my first new friend back on the mainland, which is no easy feat for me. My new pal was a chunky, two-year-old mini–Australian shepherd named Kona. She was the boss's dog and would come in with him periodically. She was a bit aloof, but I adored her.

When she was happy, her back end wiggled with such ferocity that it looked like she would helicopter off the ground, tail-nub first.

When I wasn't working, I was exploring. My passion for extended periods of time alone in the outdoors had carried over. I spent all my free time in the mountains, hiking and backpacking alone. It soothed my nervous system in a way that nothing else could. The sensory input from the busy city would make my body practically rattle and my ears ring. After these adventures, I'd return to work refreshed and excitedly recount my time in the wilderness to Steve. One day he suggested that I take Kona with me.

"Really?" I asked. "Yeah! The vet said she needs to get more exercise, and we don't have much time to spend with her these days." He and his wife were both working full time and had just had a baby boy.

I started taking Kona for some small day hikes to see how we'd do. She loved it, and I loved it. We were great together. We communicated easily, built trust quickly, and, most importantly, we had fun. I didn't have much experience with dogs at the time. There were the two that had been around when I was young, and Cooper, and of course Cerberus, but those were all pretty hands-off (except for Cerberus, which was more *hands on fire*), so I was surprised at how natural this felt.

Our day hikes quickly progressed to overnight backpack trips. I spent time researching trails and conditions, making sure that dogs were allowed, and that we'd both be capable of succeeding within the terrain. We explored the Olympics and summited peaks in the Cascades, glissading down snow chutes and playing in pristine glacial lakes. At the end of the day, we'd crawl into the tent, exhausted. Kona would snuggle up to me in a little spoon position while I covered her with a blanket, and that's how we'd wake up in the morning, renewed and ready for the next day's adventures. I was in love.

When I first started dating Johnny, we took Kona cragging. Johnny is an accomplished rock climber and wanted to show me the ropes, so to speak. Kona would stand near Johnny as he belayed me to the top of the wall, and Kona would whimper on my behalf. It is *scary*. We hiked in the dune-filled canyons, and Kona would bark at her echo. She was so silly and brought so much laughter and joy into my life.

Driving back to the city after these adventures was always hard. It was jarring to go from one environment to the other, and although I mostly enjoyed my job, I didn't feel that I had real purpose there. It was also hard to leave Kona with her family. When I'd drop her off, she'd run inside, then to the upper deck and stand howling in distress as I drove away. My heart broke every time. Steve started casually suggesting that perhaps I adopt her—like, full time. For a long while, I thought he was joking, but eventually I realized that he was serious. But I was in no position to have a dog. My living situation wasn't stable, my income wasn't stable, my emotional state was barely stable. I spoke to my parents about my dilemma. They'd been hearing all about my adventures with and connection to Kona. After some time they told me that they'd be willing to adopt Kona until I was ready to have her full time. I was overjoyed. I told Steve the great news, and the very next day I received a text from his wife that said, "I don't understand why you would want to take my dog away from me."

I was dumbfounded. I'm not sure where the communication breakdown had occurred, or whether she had simply changed her mind, but that was the abrupt and devastating end of my relationship with my boss's dog.

I think about Kona periodically, more so since my journey with Bunny began. I feel fortunate to finally be in a place where I can dedicate the time and energy necessary to fully facilitate a relationship like this, and where I don't have to leave her howling on someone else's balcony. Call me late to the party of Dog Guardianship, but these creatures are incredible. I feel like I've unlocked a new achievement and am just now recognizing its full potential.

27

An Exploration of Novelty

I looked at Bunny, who was standing by her board, then surveyed the camping equipment scattered around the living room. Sleeping bags, haul bags, tent, climbing gear, skis—we were prepared for any and all activities. I asked Bunny, "Are you excited for your first road trip, Buns?" She looked at me, then glanced at the pile of stuff, then back at me, and pressed UGH.

Every year since Johnny and I met, we take the last week of March and the first week of April to road-trip. Our primary goal is to get as far away from civilization as possible and to disconnect from the daily grind and reconnect with nature. I don't really allow myself to turn off much, so at least one two-week wilderness adventure per year is a mandatory reset, after which I am filled with renewed creativity and purpose. We took 2020 off from vacation travel because it didn't feel responsible given the COVID-19 pandemic, so in 2021 we were especially excited to be getting back out. We'd only ever spent one night in a tent with Bunny outdoors and had since upgraded from a two-person to a three-person tent to more comfortably accommodate us all.

There were so many unknowns, and Johnny and I were both a bit nervous about whether she would take to it or not. Would she bark all night in the tent at the slightest sound? Would she tolerate the rough backroads on which we'd spend most of our days? Bunny had been carsick for months when she was a puppy, and although she'd long since overcome that, she still didn't love car rides. Would she be anxious in a perpetually changing environment for two weeks? One of the concerns I didn't have was whether she'd be okay without her buttons for that long. We spent considerable time discussing the pros and cons of bringing them, but concluded that it just didn't make sense. We wouldn't be in any one place for long enough. Our days would be filled with mental stimulation and adventure, and from the start of my journey with Bunny my goal had been to have great communication with her on her terms first. We already communicate beautifully without them.

On the Monday of our departure, as we were organizing the final bits and pieces of our trip, Bunny seemed anxious. Johnny and I were behaving out of the ordinary, off a regular schedule, and that meant that she couldn't predict what would be coming next. I reassured her, saying, "We go big happy play walk." That seemed to relax her. We headed out the door, hauling our gear up the hill with Buns excitedly at our heels. She paused at the door of the truck as she regularly does. I imagined her recalling the times she was sick in the past and calculating whether or not it was safe to give the car another shot. After a moment, she reluctantly hopped in, and we were on our way.

The weather forecast told us that it would likely be cold and wet for the first day or two, and it wasn't mistaken. Our first night, we camped on snow-covered ground near a creek on federal property administered by the Bureau of Land Management. It was almost dark by the time we got there, so we played with Bunny, took a walk, then ate and quickly went to bed. She seemed initially

uneasy in the tent, especially once we zipped the doors and rainfly, but she settled down to sleep before too long. The temps dropped into the low teens that night, and despite many layers and down sleeping bags for us and a thick padded bed and blankets for Buns, we were quite cold.

In the middle of the night, Bunny let out a tiny howl that woke both Johnny and me. I'd never heard a noise like that from her before, and she seemed equally surprised. I wondered if she'd been dreaming. The next day when we talked about it, we discovered Johnny and I had both had very strange dreams. I hoped that one day Buns would be able to tell us about her peculiar dreams.

As we made our way farther south from Washington into Oregon, Bunny seemed to find a routine. Car time was for sleeping, because she had to conserve energy for all the new sounds, smells, and experiences when we'd stop. She was now jumping into the truck without hesitation and getting comfortable right away. I'd frequently look back to see her curled up in a ball, paws tucked, and say to Johnny, "Look, look how precious! I'm so proud of her!" He'd glance back, nod, and smile.

We traveled on increasingly rural roads, most of them unpaved. At one point a Border collie, crouching low in the classic fashion of its breed, effectively herded our truck to a standstill, then barked and ran off. Bunny's ears perked, and she sat up to look out the window. I know her; if she had her buttons, she would've said, "What sound? Stranger dog."

At a potty pit stop I turned around to see Bunny hopping on three legs toward me. I imagine she would have said, "Paw, ouch," as she placed her paw in my hand, and I found a goat head thorn in her pad. I plucked it out and she was right as rain again, running off to sniff a huge pile of cow patties.

We don't camp in campgrounds, choosing instead to camp on undeveloped BLM grounds as much as we can. Some of the roads we found ourselves on would've tested all but the heartiest of stomachs, but Bunny learned to lower her center of gravity and brace accordingly, if not elegantly. Only when we drove through particularly rocky gullies and washed-out roads would she look to us and smack her lips several times, letting us know that she was concerned. I'd coo softly to reassure her or offer treats, which she mostly refused.

On our way to the high desert and as many hot springs as we could find, roads were rural and rough, and services practically nonexistent. We came prepared with an extra five gallons of gasoline, a ton of water, and copious snacks. At one point, after we'd been driving for hours, Johnny looked over and said, "I have to poop." Bunny's ears perked up at her favorite word, but then she went back to sleep.

We were headed to an isolated hot spring that had eluded us when we were traveling in the Subaru Outback that Johnny had owned since 2004. But while our confidence was bolstered by the truck we now owned, the conditions were unfortunately not in our favor. After what had already been a harrowing drive, we got stuck in a mud-and-snow combination. We'd come prepared for that possibility—and unstuck ourselves quickly—but it didn't bode well for the remainder of that road as it rose in elevation. So we turned around and re-routed to a spring we knew well and loved. Did you know that there are actual rivers of hot springs in the middle of nowhere? They are streams with pools large and deep enough to fully submerge oneself. Nature absolutely blows my mind. Johnny and I soaked for a while. We kept Bunny at a safe distance, and she watched with curiosity. We camped not far from there, staying in the high desert, and that night Bunny woke us up barking. I'm not sure what she heard, and I didn't hear anything worrisome myself when I sat up to reassure her. I thought, "She'd have pressed SOUND, SETTLE, MAD." The atmosphere was bone dry, and in the pitch black as I petted her, I could see trails of static sparks following my fingers like a meteor shower.

We had another very remote hot spring in mind for our next stop. We spent most of the day driving off-road at ten miles per hour or less, and as we approached our destination we were dismayed to see six battered trucks and several men stationed right at the spring. As we drew closer, one of them started blasting death metal, as if to say, *You can come up here, but you aren't going to enjoy it.* They had hauled two dirty couches right to the mouth of the hot spring, and there were exploded fireworks and beer cans littering the ground in this High Rock Canyon Emigrant Trails National Conservation Area. Johnny and I decided to quickly look at and touch the spring since we'd come all that way, but then we departed. I was deeply saddened. The juxtaposition of pristine protected wilderness and the reckless destruction of it broke my heart. Overhearing small bits of their conversation was equally dismaying—they were comparing crack pipes. We did not feel safe and heeded our gut instinct to depart quickly. We returned to the car where Bunny was growling softly.

I suspect there is zero percent chance that any of them will ever read this, but to the white men at that natural wonder: Your vibes were a tad murdery. Please go easy on the crack. Don't set off fireworks or shoot bottles in a protected wilderness, it's destructive to the flora and fauna who live there. Using music as intimidation isn't cool, and give yourselves a shade structure for fuck's sake. You're going to get heat stroke and boil your remaining brain cells. Thank you and best wishes.

After a couple more nights in the high desert of Nevada, we headed down into California, and then up along the coast. Bunny had only ever seen our beach, which paled in comparison. With miles of wide, sandy coastline before her, there was only one logical thing to do: ZOOM. One of the greatest joys in my life is seeing unbridled happiness in my dog. I feel like a large part of my self-worth is now durably tied to her contentment. It is my mission to get her to smile. It's not the easiest task. She's a pretty serious lady. And when I can't make her smile, I feel like I've failed her. But more than this, she's allowed me to connect in a new way with my own potential joy and pain. Simply watching her breathe soothes me. A previously unoccupied space in my chest that I hadn't known existed now filled with more worry and love than I thought possible.

Watching Bunny run giant circles on the beach, occasionally spinning out as her body struggled to keep up with her legs, tongue flapping from side to side, made me feel whole in that moment.

We moved away from the coastline and found a spot to call home for the night on the ridge of a timbered crater. At sunset we walked around the rim and down through the crater. There were large flowering bushes lining the trail, swarming with pollinating bees that filled the warm air with a soothing hum. Bunny took great interest in the bear scat we came across, and in the fearless chipmunks that seemed to rule the land.

As much as my joy is tied to Bunny's, so is my anxiety. To see her in distress pains me like nothing else. This is mitigated by the fact that she has a way to express and potentially explain what bothers her, but she didn't have her tools—her buttons—with her on the last night of our trip. We chose to spend that night in a dog-friendly hotel near the beach. The place was awesome— lovely room, comfy bed, kitchenette, ocean literally at our doorstep. However, the litany of sounds coming from adjacent rooms and from the busy beach was too much for Bunny. She is already very sound sensitive, and in this new environment her anxiety rose to a boiling point. What started as intermittent sound reactivity quickly built to incessant anxious cries. She was having a panic attack. It was the only time during our trip that I felt that having the buttons may have been a benefit. Maybe she could have helped us help her. Could she have explained her feelings in a way that would have been cathartic to her? Or have told us more precisely how to comfort her? Perhaps she would simply have felt more heard. I don't know. But I do know that I've never been able to talk myself out of a panic attack. Sometimes too much is just too much, and more sensory input is not the answer. I think having the buttons there would have been more for my benefit than hers, because if she'd been capable of using them at all, then it would've meant I hadn't put her in a situation that had given her a panic attack to begin with. Johnny tried sleeping with her in the truck, away from the hotel sounds, but we all know how she feels about personal space, so that only lasted about five minutes. It wasn't until almost three a.m. that she was able to settle down enough to sleep. We woke up tired and frustrated, not at Bunny but at our inability to soothe her.

The final push home was quick and uneventful. According to her custom, Bunny slept for most of the drive. At first, her head kept slipping off the seat as she tried to position all her giraffe-like legs comfortably. She'd jolt awake with each fall and reposition herself, only to have it slide right back off. As I took my hoodie off and stuffed it in the crack to make a pillow for her, I reflected on our trip and all I'd learned about Bunny during this week on the road. This had been a novel experience for us all. Johnny and I had never traveled with Bunny like this, or for this long. Bunny had never camped or been away from the comfort of the territory she called home. So many things could have gone wrong.

Yet Buns is much braver and more adaptable than I'd expected. It is odd to me that my default belief about both her and I had been the same—that we are somehow inherently weak, fragile at our core. Incapable of withstanding change. Relentlessly confused and anxious. But that is simply not true. We are resilient and fluid. Adaptable and inexhaustibly curious. Once again, Bunny was a mirror for my own human experience that strangely hadn't been receptively reflected up until this point.

After parking the truck, we trotted down the two hundred fifty stairs to our beachside home, Bunny running with gleeful, reckless abandon ahead of us. She knew, of course, exactly where she was and where we were headed. As we walked toward the house, I wondered if she would get right back to using the buttons, or if her progress would be inadvertently slowed by being away from them for a week.

I didn't have to wonder for long. We hadn't been home for more than ten minutes before she pranced over to the board and pressed PLAY TANGO. And so we did! It was nice to be in our familiar space, but nicer to know that, for Bunny, home seemed to be wherever we were together.

28

I Dog,
Why Dog,
Who Dog,
You Dog

Before our road trip, Bunny had been using the buttons consistently and in contextually appropriate ways, but the rhythm she found excluded much exploration. She'd position herself before her NASA console (as Twitter memes like to call it) and use the words that were comfortably within her paw's reach. It felt like we had plateaued, and I wasn't sure how to encourage her to branch out.

I would spend time throughout the day thinking about what she might find interesting to talk about. What was she already telling me without words? Well, she yelled at some birds. Already had a BIRD button. She played with

Selena. Already had PLAY and SELENA buttons. We went to the PARK and to the BEACH, played BALL, had some SETTLE time with SCRITCHES. She had a large variety of buttons that I was interested in her using but that she didn't seem to care much about, and I had long since decided that I would never remove a word regardless of whether or not she was using it. After all, if one day I no longer had access to the word *tohubohu* I would be gutted, even if I rarely use it. I continued to model more abstract concepts paired with words that I knew she enjoyed using, but she was in a comfortable cadence—her needs were being met and the last thing I wanted to do was to add unnecessary pressure. Perhaps this is as far as we go, I thought to myself. And I would've been fine with that.

So I was surprised and delighted that upon our return, Bunny began exploring the buttons with a fervor and curiosity I hadn't yet seen, centered, it appeared, primarily around self-awareness and understanding. This weeklong break from her buttons seemed to give her brain the time necessary to stabilize previous information in her long-term memory, which then gave her the space and motivation to continue building upon it. I was floored as Bunny repeatedly said, I DOG then looked to me for confirmation. Then DOG WHAT and DOG WHY and I DOG WE FRIEND and MOM DOG WAS. I quickly added a HUMAN button, so she'd have a basis of comparison. The next day I pointed to the mirror and asked, "Who this?" She put her nose to the dog in the mirror, then said DOG BUNNY. A few minutes later I asked again, this time pointing to myself in the mirror. We made eye contact, then I watched in the reflection as she pressed HUMAN FRIEND. What had changed?

Studies, including *"Absolute Coding of Stimulus Novelty in the Human Substantia Nigra/VTA,"* by Nico Bunzeck and Emrah Düzel, have shown that novelty—when not paired with a perceived threat—increases levels of dopamine in our brains. This may be a direct result of evolutionary adaptation. As our brains grew, so did our capacity for learning. An attraction to novelty would have motivated us to explore more, and problem solve in new environments.

This exploration would then be rewarded by a dose of dopamine and a higher likelihood that we would thrive. Several genetic studies have also linked divergent or creative thinking and dopamine neurotransmission.

In my personal experience, novelty, though initially overwhelming, still leaves me with renewed enthusiasm and inspiration. Some of the biggest breakthroughs in my own art practice came after a period of underinspired rhythm, when I was thrust (not always by choice) into a totally new situation or environment. After the novel experience, my creativity would be free-flowing once again. This was certainly the case for me after I returned from our road trip, and it seemed to have been the case for Bunny as well.

The animals that cohabitate with us tend to live very sheltered lives. They often don't get to see much other than their daily walking routes and their regular caregivers. They don't have much autonomy, with their outside lives mostly lived on leashes tethered to us. And often these walks we take them on are more about us, so we tug them along because we are impatient for them to do their business so we can get home, or we're trying to get our steps in. And we have an expectation that they will obey blindly. We correct them for displaying absolutely normal dog behavior if it doesn't suit us. They stay in kennels while we travel, are bathed when we make them, are occasionally forced into clothes for their warmth or our pleasure, and often eat the same food every day forever. They are rarely afforded the freedom to express natural behaviors. Most importantly, they do not get a say in anything and are not allowed to say no to us.

Obviously, this is a gross generalization, but maybe you see where this is going. We took a road trip, and every single thing Bunny saw, heard, and smelled for a week was novel. I can't begin to fathom what that must have been like for her. In the year and a half she'd been in our lives, I'd exposed her to as many new environments, sounds, animals, tastes, textures, and people as possible—as part of proper socialization—but, inevitably, we fell into a routine. The trip would've been amazing regardless, but it was made so much more beautiful thinking about what it might have meant to her. Is it any surprise that she returned a philosopher?

Witnessing Bunny's new curiosity and speech patterns was so inspiring that I decided I would take her on another trip a couple of months later. I booked a rental on the Washington coast, near a beach that had long held sentimental value to me. I'd spent many hours there, walking for miles, searching for agates, petrified wood, and sand dollars. It is a place where I can center myself. And this time, I would bring her buttons to see whether she'd use them at all in this new location.

We left Tacoma on Mother's Day morning and arrived too early to check in, so we went directly to the beach. I knew the road well, and the smell as we drew closer was so familiar and comforting. I already knew that Bunny loves beaches. This was going to be great! We frolicked for a couple of hours, Buns played for a bit with another dog we met, and then we made our way to our rental. I was surprised at how long it took us to get there from the beach, as the listing had said we were walking distance. We arrived at the small house in a residential area. There was a turkey wandering around in the neighbor's yard and some kids playing in a sprinkler across the street. I unloaded the car, gave Bunny some food and water, and got right to reassembling her board. The HexTiles separate from one another, and stack neatly in foam carrying cases that prevent the buttons from activating during travel. That last part only kind of works as I'd periodically heard CONCERNED and POOP coming from the back of the car on our drive. I'd taken a photograph of the board just before we left to be sure that I reassembled them in exactly the same order, although I probably could have done it from memory.

There was one bed downstairs and a small loft upstairs with three beds packed in, surfer-bungalow style. It was a chilly evening, and I noticed that all the thermostats were nonfunctioning. I grabbed an extra blanket from the closet and threw it on the bed I'd chosen. It was at that point that I noticed

lemon-size blood stains on the foldover sheet. *Hmm,* I thought, *this isn't ideal.* I looked at Bunny and said, "Let's go back downstairs." I took a seat on the couch and opened my computer to do a bit of work.

Bunny stared at me earnestly, then walked around her board and pressed MOM BYE. "Oh you wanna go back home?" I said, trying to convince myself that I didn't. She paused, stared at me, then pressed COME DAD. "Dad's not coming. It's just you and me baby," I replied.

We can do this, I thought to myself—but it seemed we were sharing a sentiment that, at least on my end, was unspoken, and I'm thankful she was able to express it. We made the most of two nights and three days there but ended up leaving early. She used her board while we were there about as consistently as she did at home, but it seemed more frantic and less calculated. I saw more stress signals in us both. The positive effect of the novelty, it turned out, was hugely contingent on environment, and this was not the right environment for us.

Clever Hans

Okay. Buckle up. This one's a real bummer and arguably put an end to animal language studies being taken seriously for a long time. Bunny and I get compared to this story all the damn time, and yeah, I get it. I really do. The pursuit of knowledge is rife with catastrophic failures and sad ends. Even the most beautiful examples of sentience and communicative intent are ripped to scientific shreds—which I suppose I understand, in the name of science, but it still feels like we're somehow missing the bigger picture.

Clever Hans was a horse that lived in the first decade of the twentieth century. His trainer was a mathematician by the name of Wilhelm von Osten, who claimed to have taught Hans to perform arithmetic operations, read clocks, spell in German, identify artists by their works, and other such astounding feats. Even more impressive, Hans could perform these feats in front of large audiences. The German Board of Education was naturally skeptical and ran a series of tests over the course of a year and a half, wherein they separated Hans from von Osten to see if his skills could be replicated. Much to their surprise, they found no evidence of trickery. Hans consistently performed with high levels of accuracy, even in the absence of von Osten.

Still dubious, the commission enlisted the help of psychologist Oskar Pfungst, who performed blind tests, where the questioner was out of sight and therefore could not inadvertently cue Hans, as well as tests where the questioner did not already know the answer. In these instances, Hans performed about as well as I might when asked to perform complicated mathematical tasks, which is to say, not well at all. It's not necessarily that Hans wasn't a genius, he was just a genius of the "reading subtle facial and body cues of those around him" variety. Which, to be fair, is the category of genius most animals fall into.

To me, the lesson within this story is that language is not the be-all and end-all, but that clear and beautiful communication exists with or without it. For the scientific community, the lesson was that studies such as these should rigorously avoid face-to-face contact for the sake of experimental sterilization. The value of studies conducted since with gray parrots, dogs, dolphins, and other animals using face-to-face learning have been hotly contested, citing Hans as evidence that inquiries such as these have no scientific legitimacy.

Not to be the bearer of bad news, but if you weren't a fan of how Hans's story started, you're really going to hate how it ended. Hans fell from grace once the world found out that he wasn't a genius in the way we expected him to be, and suffered an extremely sad end at the beginning of World War I when he was drafted as a military horse and either killed in action or eaten by hungry soldiers. Wtf.

29

Along Came Otter

When Bunny was about a year old, I started imagining a future with two dogs in our lives, but I was in no rush. I was still learning so much about Bunny, about myself, about behavior. I'd noticed that Bunny was reactive and had dog-selective tendencies (i.e., a sort of pickiness about what dogs she was comfortable being approached by). Some dogs, for example, are only comfortable interacting with dogs of their own size or sex. Bunny's least favorite dogs are small brachycephalic breeds like pugs and Boston terriers. Also, this is actually a thing. Many dogs are uneasy around brachys due to their unconventional posture and the unusual sounds they often make. Bunny was forging a path forward that would allow her to live her best life in spite of these challenges. And I was setting more and better boundaries, speaking with more trainers and behaviorists, and educating myself constantly. I knew it wouldn't be easy if—or when—we decided to bring a second dog home, but I also knew that once Bunny decided someone was "friend" she was solidly bonded. I'd watched how positive her relationship with Selena was and seen how when Selena was around, Bunny became less reactive. I wondered if another dog, with the right temperament and calculated introductions, could have a similar effect on her. And there I was, actively seeking information with which to make an informed decision, while not actively planning to immediately add to our family, when all of a sudden the perfect puppy nearly fell into my lap.

His name was Otter. He was a standard poodle with a dream temperament from a responsible breeder in Boise. Medium drive, bombproof (i.e., nonreactive and resilient), sweet, curious, and whip smart. I'd looked into fostering, but with no yard, two cats, and a reactive dog, my chances of being approved were slim, and I was really concerned about the possibility of introducing a second set of behavioral issues from a dog who might have been traumatized by the system or prior experiences. One reactive dog was enough. I Facetimed with Otter's breeder, Nicole, and we had a very long talk. He was ready to come home in a week, and if it hadn't been for the work I was already doing with Bunny, I wouldn't have been a contender to become his next caretaker. A quick decision had to be made, and I followed my gut, my research, and Johnny's okay. The combination of these things has rarely led me astray. "Let's do it!" I said, and began frantically prepping my home for the new addition, mentally preparing management strategies for his arrival.

I joyfully announced my decision the next day on Instagram and was met with the congratulatory responses from followers eager to watch this integration unfold. Would Otter learn how to use the buttons from watching Bunny, as Kanzi had from his mother? How long would it take Bunny to call him "family"? Would she stop using the buttons altogether? These were all possibilities that I had considered. I was also met with an alarming and unexpected amount of pushback (I should have expected it at this point, but I never do) from the "adopt don't shop" community. People are entitled to their opinions,

but when I say pushback, I mean name-calling and threats. Not acceptable. I'm told that it comes with the territory, the internet being the internet, but I'll never get used to it. I spent several days in tears during what should have been a joyous occasion. My brain told me, "Man up, you're too sensitive, you're just going to have to get used to it"—except I shouldn't have to. The internet sucks. It's also wonderful, but as Bunny would say . . . *ugh*.

I've got to be honest, I struggled with whether to adopt or to purchase from a breeder. All three of our cats were adopted, and I loved them dearly. There are so many unethical breeders, out to make a quick buck off "trending" dogs, and in my research before Bunny I contacted several who I quickly learned fell into that category. It was disheartening. Similarly, I read many stories of shelters misrepresenting the temperament of adoptable dogs just to move them out of the facility, only to have them back there six months down the road when the adopters realized that they didn't have the skills necessary to tackle the behavioral challenges they were seeing. Of course, the opposite is also true in both cases. It's a complicated issue. In my case, knowing Bunny's temperament and quirks, I wanted as much as possible to be able to anticipate drive and temperament. I wanted a dog that came from lines without human or dog aggression. Without resource-guarding tendencies or separation anxiety. I knew that Bunny could adapt and would thrive with the right dog, and I wasn't willing to gamble. And of course, even best laid plans go awry—but at least by purchasing a dog from a reputable breeder, I had a guarantee that if for some reason things didn't work out, she would take the dog back without question. I 100 percent agree that if people can adopt, yes, it's a really important step in helping to reduce the unwanted, uncared-for animal population. But each person or family has to make the choice that's right for them.

I flew to Boise on the first of August to pick the little dude up. I was nervous, just like I was when I went to get Bunny, except this time it was for somewhat different reasons. I hadn't met Otter yet, and the anxiety about the integration of a new pup into our established routine was top of mind. Another woman from the Seattle area was on the flight picking up one of Otter's brothers. On the way back we were able to swap seats so that our puppies were side by side. The fluffy little noodles didn't make a peep.

I'd spoken to trainer and behavior consultant friends about how best to approach the meeting and first few months of life, and all of them advised taking it slowly given Bunny's spicy temperament. Some trainers don't let existing dogs interact with new dogs for six months. They'd crate and rotate or keep the puppy in a separate room while both dogs had a chance to acclimate to the new smells and sounds. It's easier to foster a healthy relationship slowly than to fix one that develops conflict from moving too fast. I hoped that Bunny wouldn't take that long to acclimate, but I was prepared for a long period of management.

There is a small, oddly shaped nook underneath the stairs in our living room. The previous tenants had used it for their kid's sleepovers—the perfect cavelike fort vibe. As soon as we moved in we set it up to serve as Bunny's space, but she always chose the couch by her buttons instead, so we decided Otter would be a more reliable tenant. We put a pet bed and many more toys than he needed in it, then gated the opening with a wire pen covered by a blanket as a visual barrier. My goal was subthreshold desensitization. This threshold is the mental limitation under which a dog can still think, but over which the sympathetic nervous system kicks in and they're all fight, flight, or freeze. No more thinking. This is when bad decisions happen, so we always try to stay under that threshold, myself included. I knew that if we could avoid negative interactions from the beginning and let them get used to each other's presence slowly, the path forward would be smoother. The only time they interacted for the first week was outside when we would walk together as a family. I would walk Bunny and Johnny would walk Otter. They were short walks because Otter was still tiny, but every time we did this I could see Bunny's body soften a little bit.

While we were home, I made sure to spend individual time with each of them. There'd be scritches, chats, and play with Bunny, then she would go upstairs and hang out in my office while I trained and played with Otter, building our bond and communication and getting to know one another. During one of my training sessions with Otter, he peed on Bunny's buttons. Yikes. We were doing really well with potty training, but I'd waited too long for his next trip outside. I immediately took Otter out to show him again where appropriate potty activity happened, then cleaned up the mess as best I could. Two of the buttons had been soaked and now made a garbled nonsensical sound, so I replaced them. Okay, all good, I thought, then went about my business.

Bunny didn't use her buttons much those first few days. Otter's arrival was a huge shift, and she was understandably preoccupied. The next day, however, she adamantly pressed POTTY POTTY POTTY. "Okay, let's go potty," I said. We walked outside, I went out the gate and down the steps, and waited for her to follow. She looked at me quizzically, whimpered softly, then trotted back inside. "That must have been a mistake," I thought. So I went back inside and sat back down to work.

Moments later I again hear POTTY POTTY. "Hmmm, okay. Let's try again,

I guess." Again, I walked outside and waited for her to follow. This time, she stayed at her board, eyes fixed on me, unmoving. I walked back in and asked her, "Do you want to go potty?" She pressed POTTY again, then bent to sniff the tiles that Otter had defiled. "Ohhhhhhhh," I said, remembering a dog's nose is a bajillion times more sensitive than mine. "Yikes, yeah. I'm sorry, dude." I replaced the whole affected tile segment, and then we were back in business.

After about a week, during one of our parallel walks, Johnny and I let Bunny and Otter off leash to allow them some interaction if they chose it. My heart swelled as I saw cautious play-bows, spins, and playful energy. We were making progress. Shortly thereafter we allowed them to play on the deck a little bit. Bunny bounded around excitedly, while Otter kept an attentive distance. We kept playdates like this short and sweet, ending them at the slightest sign of overarousal. During one such session, Otter, who'd gained some confidence, jumped up and grabbed Bunny's cheek fur and indelicately began tugging her across the room. I immediately moved to step in, but Bunny corrected him appropriately with a quick snap. Puppies are annoying.

Bunny was back to using the buttons regularly within a few days, and, unsurprisingly, most of her conversations revolved around Otter. She was spending lots of time observing him. One day, after standing at his covered gate, tail wagging, she walked to her buttons and pressed the query button (imagine a sort of swooping sound that rises in pitch). ??? ??? COME. She looked toward Otter, then back to the buttons and pressed, WHERE LOOK PLAY.

"You want play Otter?" I asked. She wagged her tail and walked in the direction of his room. After a short play session between the two of them, I put Otter in his safe space behind the gate for a nap. Bunny walked to her buttons and pressed IS HELP SETTLE. "Yes, Buns, Otter settle now."

I got overconfident and removed the blanket covering the gate the next day. But complete eye contact between the two dogs proved to be overstimulating and resulted in a bit of fixation on Bunny's part. A hard stare, stiff posture, lifted paw, and a lip lick were all signs that Bunny was quickly becoming uncomfortable, so back up went the blanket while we attempted to keep everything subthreshold. The road may not be quick for Otter and Bunny, and that's okay. My own journey has been unendingly winding and full of roadblocks the size of Everest, and if I'm being honest, although easy sounds nice, it also sounds boring. What do we learn from easy?

30

The Secret

This way. Good girl!" I say cheerily as Bunny U-turns and follows me away from one of the fast-approaching, off-leash dogs we frequently encounter on the beach by our home. Otter stops to greet the other dog. I say, "Otter, come," and he trots over with aplomb. As is commonplace here, I don't see a human associated with the dog, and I know the dog's name . . . it's Rally. I love her. She's a tiny spitfire Brittany spaniel about the same age as Otter. She's the wiggliest. Bunny hates her, but Bunny dislikes all puppies, really. They're rude and don't know how to dog. Little humans are much the same, I find. Loud, unpredictable, and without dog-sense. There are lots of those around here too.

It's one of the special things about this community—that dogs and children are safe to wander. Everyone knows everyone, and we are contained by cliffs and water. However, as obsessed as I am with our unique little throwback microcosm, it is far from an ideal environment for Bunny. To get from our home to my car involves a fifteen-minute walk, the first half of which is on a narrow boardwalk behind the houses. Steep cliffs on one side, tidal water on the other. There's no street to cross away from someone Bunny doesn't like, and even my best management skills can't compete with such little passing room and an off-leash dog running toward us. The final stretch to the parking lot after the boardwalk is a steep two hundred fifty stairs, with even less passing room. We were running the gauntlet every time we wanted to go for a walk. Sometimes we'd be four spicy reactions deep before we even got to the stairs. I didn't know what to do. There wasn't an alternative route, and I could tell that we were both becoming increasingly tense in anticipation of these walks. Both of us perpetually trigger stacked, one of us now in a muzzle and the other in tears, feeling like a failure as a dog guardian.

Around this time, my research into behavior had turned to ethology. It felt more holistic and was somehow freeing to view what I had considered challenging behaviors as evolutionary, adaptive traits rather than flaws or failures. Bunny's behaviors began to make more sense within this context, and unsurprisingly, so did mine.

I'd taken Kim Brophey's course in applied ethology and was thinking a lot about the impact of environment on behavior. We all know that a change of environment can change your mood. It's the reason getting out of town helps us reset. A break from the habitual can allow our neural pathways to reroute. It's why quitting smoking, for example, is easier when you've just moved or changed jobs.

One fall day in 2021, I was in tears after a particularly challenging walk. Sure, it's stressful for me, having a reactive dog, but mostly I just felt sad for Bunny. Can you imagine having a panic attack every time you saw another human? That's what it was like, and that sounds fucking awful. I turned to Johnny and said, "We need our own trail to the parking lot." Then louder and with more conviction, "We should make our own trail to the parking lot!" (Not a thing that seemed at all like a legitimate option.) To my surprise and glee, Johnny thought for a moment and said, "We should."

We spent the next six months slowly and secretly carving switchbacks up the cliff, through a sea of poison oak, downed trees, and Himalayan blackberry, and taking great care not to remove plants that would affect the stability of the slope and leave us vulnerable to landslides. Sometimes, Bunny and Otter would even come with us as we worked. Bunny watched us with concern. Otter helped us dig and zoomed recklessly through the underbrush.

By spring we had our own steep, squirrelly, but usable trail to the parking lot, from which we could access all our favorite wooded trails. And we had effectively eliminated Bunny's reactions, giving her cortisol levels a chance to drop, which meant that even when we did encounter another dog or stranger, she was better prepared to handle the moment without a reaction. We stopped needing her muzzle. I cried less.

This adjustment to our environment falls squarely in the management category. I wasn't trying to actively modify her behavior. But it did, in fact, positively modify both Bunny's and my behavior.

Behavior modification is inherently manipulative, and it's something that I've grappled with increasingly throughout our relationship. It's not all bad, obviously, but behavior exists for a reason. It is not my mission to make Bunny more pliable or obedient for my comfort, but to enable her to experience life without so much stress. This process was about determining the why of her behavior, and then adjusting external factors in a way that allowed change to happen naturally, passively. Less invasively or despotically. It's a process that feels kind to me. In line with a sort of radical acceptance both of others and self. An acknowledgment of a meeting in the middle. A true partnership.

31

Bunny and the Grands, or Road Trip, Part Deux

get annoyed with myself when people ask how exactly I've taught Bunny to communicate with buttons, because I want to have this really smart answer and sometimes I can piece together something that sounds halfway decent, but in my head I'm always saying, "I dunno. I just did." But then, I wouldn't be me if I didn't take every opportunity to undersell myself. It wasn't until we left Bunny for a week with my parents that it started to become clear how much effort I'd actually dedicated to her development.

Spring break 2022 was fast approaching, and Johnny and I set to planning our road trip, like we do. Otter was almost a year old. I'd learned a ton about him since he'd been with us, but Otter being part of the family also taught me a lot about Bunny. I knew by now that Otter wanted to see and do everything

(like me at times), and I was beginning to understand that Bunny preferred her world to be small, predictable, and cozy (also like me at times). I'd never imagined a dog saying no to walks before, yet here Bunny was snubbing the very idea of going outside with both body and words. I didn't trust her first verbal no to a walk, and I think she only did it because I hadn't listened to her nonverbal nos. But when I asked a second time, she turned and walked away from me, clumsily curling up in the farthest corner of the couch and closing her eyes. *All*

right then, I thought. *No walk for you.* She is very much a dog of leisure, and as such we decided that for this road trip, Otter would come adventure with us and Bunny would stay with my parents, enjoying slow, garden-filled days and lots of tasty treats.

My stomach was in my throat as I set up the buttons and a camera in my parents' living room. I felt so guilty leaving Bunny, even though I'd gone out of my way to make sure she was comfortable with my parents and the space. I'd spent a week there with both her and Otter. And Bunny *was* comfortable there, and she adored my mum and dad. We were absolutely doing what was in the best interest of Bunny's mental health. But I still cried. I forgot to say good-bye to my mum as I slipped out the door waving to Bunny, telling her how much I loved her and that we'd be back soon.

The road trip itself was rad. More far-off places, remote hot springs, high-desert shenanigans. The usual. Otter was easy. He took to sleeping in the tent quickly, and smiled pretty much nonstop, except for when he got into that fight with a tumbleweed. He won in the end and was all smiles again in no time.

Although we were out of cell range for most of our trip, we'd drive through patches of reception and my phone would ding. My parents would have inevitably sent me an adorable update and pic. "Buns gardened with me," "Buns is watching tennis with us," "Buns greets me with a 'sit pretty' every morning," "Buns is talking, but I can't hear what she's saying." (My dad wears a hearing aid, but only in one ear, even though he can't hear out of either.) These updates allowed me to relax and really enjoy my time with Johnny and Otter. Otter is an easy dog with tons of energy, and he was exactly where he wanted to be. Bunny, by comparison, is not an easy dog in most novel situations, because she doesn't like them. So her staying with my parents was perfect for her. But also, if you have a hard dog that *does* love your hobbies, it's still okay to take time for yourself.

This was the longest I'd been away from Bunny. My parents told me that as our truck crept up their driveway on our way home, Bunny knew something was up. She was whimpering and wiggling at their door, and as we opened it, she did figure eights around our legs while piddling a little on the floor out of excitement. It was great to see her, and my mum said she was sad to see her go. They'd had a lovely staycation together.

My dad had been texting me time stamps when Buns used the buttons, so that I could refer back to the recorded footage when we were home. Watching the footage opened my eyes to exactly how much time I intentionally set aside to be present for her button use. It is indeed *active listening*. I position myself close enough to the buttons that I can hear what happens if she uses them. Since her use of the buttons is mostly self-directed, I make myself available to listen, respond, and react—occasionally to the detriment of other activities. Well, frequently to their detriment, if I'm being honest. This was easiest that first year of the COVID-19 pandemic, when the whole world had slowed and I really didn't have that much else to do. People say that Bunny is unique in the way that she uses buttons, but I think a lot of that is simply her anxiety and my single-mindedness. Being heard is especially important if the world around you feels scary all the time. And if, like me, you have no life to speak of outside of your transient hyperfocuses, and happen to have a sensitive pup, you too could have an existential dog.

Watching Bunny try to communicate with buttons to my mum and dad, who did not know the layout, didn't know what the individual words sounded like, and, for the most part, couldn't hear them when they were pressed was frustrating for me. Additionally, my parents were often distracted by a television tennis match or Wordle. Then, if they did hear the buttons, they didn't know how to respond verbally or which buttons to press, or how long to wait, or how slowly to speak. All these actions have become intrinsic to me. And I could see suddenly that all of them take significant effort, focus, and sacrifice.

Bunny's button presses didn't make sense to my parents in the same way that communicating with my three-and-a-half-year-old nephew can be challenging for me. My sister-in-law can easily translate for him. My nephew and his mother have developed their own sort of language. Well, technically it's English, but it's a soft and exploratory version of English. Sounds that could be words that aren't quite, but that fill a gap within a context that gives them all the meaning they need. Like a secret language with a best friend. Like finishing your partner's sentences. Like ontogenetic ritualization.

Despite these challenges, Buns made herself understood. And Bunny herself never seemed too frustrated. And there were incredibly sweet moments when Bunny seemed to introduce herself to my dad. I'd added buttons for my parents (JOHN and JULIE) months before, and now, shortly after arriving at my parents' house, she walked to the board, pressed BUNNY JOHN, and stared up at my dad. My dad turned around upon hearing his name. He stood up and

gleefully exclaimed "John? I'm John! I'm John. JOHN!" He said it again, pointing to himself and walking around the board to be closer to Bunny. "Bunny," he said, pointing at her, and then "Julie" while gesturing in the direction of my mother. Bunny wagged her tail and trotted happily over to my mum as my dad chuckled.

In a moment that I believe thoroughly impressed both my mum and dad, Bunny walked to a pile of dirty bed sheets my mum had deposited at the top of the stairs to be washed, sniffed for a few moments, then trotted to her board to press SMELL SLEEP. "YES!" my mum exclaimed. "Smell sleep!" My dad, realizing what had just happened, wheezed with delight.

I guess what I'm trying to say is that finally *getting* it is pretty special. Being heard and understood is crucial, but doing the understanding is equally magical. It doesn't come without some persistence and a bit of sacrifice, but that feels like a no-brainer trade-off when you realize you're literally in partnership with a nonhuman.

32

The Fudgesicle

Bunny likes to talk about human poop. Otter likes to eat it. Or, to perfectly summarize their individual essences, Bunny is a shit talker while Otter has a shit-eating grin.

I first learned this horrifying parallel on the spring break road trip with Johnny and Otter, while Bunny stayed with my parents at their garden oasis, cabin in the woods. We were about a week into our trip, deep in Bureau of Land Management, high-desert ranch land looking for a spot to crash for the night. It was dark, so as soon as we found a flat spot not covered in sage brush and big enough for us to pitch a small tent, we took it. Having dialed in our systems, all three of us were cozy and fast asleep within minutes.

Sunlight hit the tent in the early morning, reminding me how cold I'd been during the night. It must've dropped into the twenties. I let Otter out of the tent, bundled up, and started making coffee on the tail bed of our truck. Only now in the light of day was I able to assess our surroundings. We'd most certainly found a previously used camp spot. There were the remains of a fire, and bullet casings littered the ground. I noticed a deer leg and was surprised that Otter hadn't immediately found it. "Dead thing" was, after all, his preferred flavor. Speaking of which, where was Otter? I scanned the landscape and caught a glimpse of him over by a pile of rocks and something . . . white? I called his name and he came gleefully running toward me with something in his mouth that looked like a chunk of wood. Not unusual for Otter to find and gnaw on a tasty tree bit. He proudly placed it in my hand. "That's funny-looking wood," I thought. It was then that I realized that this wood was slowly melting in my hand, and that it was in fact not wood at all, but frozen poop. The crappiest fudgesicle of all time.

That flash of white I mentioned earlier . . . it was toilet paper. I didn't put the pieces together until I was holding poop. I screamed and hucked the turd into the air. Johnny came rushing out of the tent to see what all the fuss was about. Otter promptly retrieved the turd and delivered it, once again to my hand, which I pulled away at the last second, resulting in it being smashed indelicately against my chest. It fell to the ground with a soft thud. I knew I had to get it away from Otter or things were going to get shittier. I went to kick it as far as I could, not realizing that it had a decent melt going on by now, so my shoe was met with less resistance and was instead absorbed by the poop. So now my shoe, shirt, and hands were covered in a stranger's poop, which Otter was now consuming with glee. R.I.P. our baby wipes and hand sanitizer. We'd remembered to pack plenty, but it turned out "plenty" was not nearly enough. We were hours from

civilization, and we weren't even headed that way. We spent the next several hours in the truck with Otter's hot turd breath on the back of our necks.

I wish I could say this was an isolated incident. After all, how often does one encounter human poop that isn't one's own (assuming you don't have a baby)? Almost never, right? Wrong.

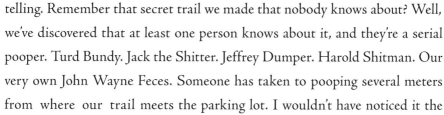

I probably don't need more than one anecdote here to illustrate my point, not that there is a point. Really, I just need more folks to carry the burden of this knowledge with me. But thanks to the absurdity of our more recent poopscapades, an additional tale bears telling. Remember that secret trail we made that nobody knows about? Well, we've discovered that at least one person knows about it, and they're a serial pooper. Turd Bundy. Jack the Shitter. Jeffrey Dumper. Harold Shitman. Our very own John Wayne Feces. Someone has taken to pooping several meters from where our trail meets the parking lot. I wouldn't have noticed it the

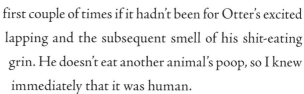

first couple of times if it hadn't been for Otter's excited lapping and the subsequent smell of his shit-eating grin. He doesn't eat another animal's poop, so I knew immediately that it was human.

If that wasn't evidence enough, just the other day as we were headed up for our walk, Otter alerted me to a pile of shit-stained toilet paper. Potentially an entire roll of it. There was a lot. With a glint in his eye, and me screaming "Noooooooooooooo!" in slow motion, he grabbed a mouthful of it and shook, sending shit shrapnel flying everywhere, while I took cover behind a tree. But here's the

clincher. Not only was there a massive pile of used toilet paper, there was also a pair of boxer briefs, shredded almost beyond recognition, which means our perp is either a werewolf with decent hygiene or the Hulk.

There's something brain breaking about a gorgeous poodle in a properly historical, Continental cut smiling at you with shit on his lips. It reminds us that for as seriously as we take ourselves, the universe has a tendency to shit on propriety, keeping our egos in check at every turd . . . er . . . turn.

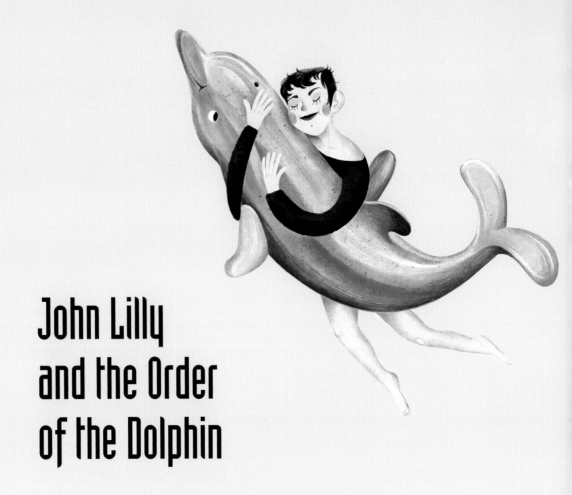

John Lilly
and the Order
of the Dolphin

The stars of this story are John Lilly, an American neuroscientist, Margaret Howe Lovatt, an animal lover, and Peter, an adolescent dolphin who lived in a research laboratory on the Caribbean Island of St. Thomas. I know I said that Clever Hans was a bummer of a story, but this one is just as sad and far more strange, so fasten your seat belts.

A NASA-funded project in the 1960s that went terribly wrong, this study was initiated to determine what challenges might be encountered when attempting to communicate with extraterrestrial life forms. That's the first red flag.

The study of dolphin intelligence was new and had become something of a cult. Lilly was a pioneer in his belief that dolphins possess higher intelligence not unlike our own, and he secured funding in his quest to prove it. Lilly, Carl Sagan, and other notable public figures of the time joined a secret society known as the Order of the Dolphin. It was very "so long and thanks for all the fish."

Margaret joined the team as a research assistant and quickly suggested that she spend twenty-four hours a day with Peter to better her chances of successfully teaching him human speech. Despite having no scientific background, Margaret seemed adept at observing and recording animal behavior. Lilly agreed, and they flooded part of the dolphin house, creating a larger and more immersive environment where Margaret and Peter could live, sleep, eat, work, and play together full time. While minimal progress was made in Peter creating humanlike utterances, he and Margaret were developing a "special" bond. As he approached sexual maturity, physiological needs began to get in the way of lesson time, so Margaret began relieving his urges manually. "It was sexual on his part. It was not sexual on mine, sensuous perhaps," she said of the experience. This *cannot get* any weirder, right? Spoiler: it does.

Lilly was introduced to LSD by the wife of Ivan Tors, the producer of the television series *Flipper*, and he became more interested personally and professionally in exploring the medicinal benefits of psychedelics than of language acquisition in dolphins. Then he wondered what effect LSD might have on his animal subjects and began to inject them with it. Lilly's concern with the welfare of the dolphins was questioned. The lab director, Gregory

Bateson (ex-husband of anthropologist Margaret Mead), and his wife, whose joint research at the facility was focused on determining how dolphins communicate among one another in the wild, left the project, and Lilly's program was defunded.

Shortly thereafter the dolphins were moved to a small lab in Florida, and within two weeks Lovatt received a call from Lilly telling her that Peter had become increasingly depressed and had died by suicide. How does a dolphin commit suicide? Well, they aren't automatic air breathers as we are, so if life becomes insufferable, they simply sink to the bottom and don't take that next breath.

The unbearable tragedy of ego, the driving ideology of human supremacy, and a sickening lack of empathy is evident in this case, as well as in so many other animal language experiments. And the credibility of research into the subject took another enormous hit.

The lesson learned? In Lilly's own words several years later, "I had no right to confine them, to imprison them, to work on them. My only right would be to work *with* them in their natural habitat, in their natural state." He later became an active participant in campaigning against animals in captivity. Huzzah . . . I guess.

The dolphin language studies of the past were thankfully not all this *Black Mirror*. In fact, one of the behavior consultants we see every now and then, Kathy Sdao, taught sign language to dolphins as a research assistant at the University of Hawaii's Kewalo Basin Marine Mammal Laboratory, run by Louis Herman. His team and their subsequent one hundred sixty or so scientific papers are responsible for most of what we now know regarding dolphin intelligence, including an assessment that dolphins have an intrinsic understanding of grammatical structure based on the accuracy with which they responded to signed sentences.

Another key player in the world of dolphin cognition is Dr. Diana Reiss.

She developed an underwater keyboard that the dolphins could press. Each button had a synthesized whistle that was paired with something the dolphins wanted—a ball, fish, or belly rubs, for example. The dolphins learned very quickly to mimic the whistles to request items and to combine them in novel ways within their own communications among themselves.

Reiss was also the first to prove that dolphins are self-aware by administering the mirror self-awareness test. Her research goes hand in hand with activism, using her reach and community to advocate for more humane practices everywhere. And I think she captures the essence of what I've tried to do with Bunny in an interview from 2014, saying, "I think the more you work with animals, you realize that the more you let them show you what the next steps are, the better."

33

What's in a Dream?

I've always had the wildest dreams. Vivid and recurring, sometimes lasting for years, with evolving characters, plotlines, landscapes, and lessons learned. During particularly rough periods in my life, I could always look forward to continuing the previous night's adventures and was able to manifest unique plotlines simply by imagining them as I drifted off to sleep. I've also been a lifelong sleep talker and occasional sleepwalker. For a long time, I recorded my nightly utterances and was always amazed and amused by the things I would say. When I lived in Italy, I shared a room with a girl my own age who would also talk in her sleep. Sometimes we would awake in the early hours of the morning to her mother barging into the room telling us to "shut up and go to sleep" in her thick Neapolitan dialect. We would look at each other, stunned. Turns out we were having sleep conversations. We were never able to convince her mother of this fact and were constantly in trouble because of it.

You know who else talks in their sleep? Chimpanzees. Or rather, chimpanzees that have been taught ASL have been known to sign in their sleep. Washoe signed *coffee*, for one. Me too, buddy. Me too. Birds as well have been known to rehearse melodies while they snooze, storing the neuronal firing pattern of the song during the day and perhaps cementing its place there during sleep.

I've sung songs in my sleep too. I've screamed in my sleep, kicked and punched in my sleep, taken orders at a restaurant in my sleep, trained Bunny in my sleep, spoken in other languages in my sleep, flown innumerable times swiftly through the forest where I grew up. What an incredible thing a dream is. As such, I love to watch dogs sleeping: the soft boofs, twitching paws, wagging tail, grumbles, and growls that one assumes are attached to dreams relating to their daily existence in the ways that ours are. Could their dreams also encapsulate unknowns? Things they haven't experienced? Monsters, creative landscapes? Are their dreams a primarily visual experience as ours are, or do they dream in sounds and smells? Is Bunny dreaming of me while I dream of her?

MIT's Center for Learning and Memory conducted a four-year study, initially focused on memory, during which they tracked the brain waves of rats doing various tasks using a device that looks at the patterns of neurons firing within the hippocampus, the part of the brain responsible for memory. After also observing the rats asleep, they noticed that the activity was identical, leading them to speculate that the activities performed by the rats during the day were being repeated while they slept. Science suggests that replaying daily events in dreams can help solidify memories and reinforce recently learned information.

Several times in interviews I've been asked, "What is your end goal?" and "What sort of conversations do you want to have with Bunny in the coming years?" My response is always, of course, that my end goal is deep connection and communication in as many ways as possible, but I started adding that I thought it would be amazing if she could one day tell me about her dreams. I never really considered it a possibility, but neither did I consider the possibility of having "conversations" with my dog at all—and yet, here we are. So when Bunny one day pressed NIGHT TALK SLEEP, then NIGHT NIGHT IS TALK TALK, then TALK IS NIGHT, I was flummoxed. I asked Johnny whether I'd been talking in my sleep, and he told me I hadn't. This went on for a couple of days, Bunny pressing NIGHT IS TALK and NIGHT TALK SLEEP. As I frequently do when I am unable to make sense of persistent utterances, I turned to the researchers, who rather quickly suggested that she might be referring to a dream. *Nah. Whaaaat?* I thought. One of the research assistants proposed that I gently wake her from a dream and ask her "what talk sleep?" to test the theory.

A few days later, I was working in my living room. Bunny was lying peacefully on the cool stone floor when she started twitching and whimpering loudly. The whimpering transitioned into muffled barks. I walked over to her and as gently as I could put my hand on her side. She awoke quickly, looking confused, and I asked her, "What talk sleep?" We walked to her board together where she pressed STRANGER ANIMAL, then stared off into the distance for a long while. As has been the case many times during my journey with Bunny, my brain nearly melted.

About a week later, shortly after we'd woken up, I asked Bunny, "What dream when sleep?" YES DOG DOG, she responded. "You dream dog when sleep?" I continued. CAT ANIMAL, Bunny replied. That tracks, I thought. And a few days after that, Bunny was standing pensively at the board when she pressed DREAM. "What did Bunny dream?" I asked. ??? DREAM TALK, she said, then DREAM WHERE DREAM. I was a bit confused, so I asked her, "Did you dream upstairs? Did you dream sleep? What did Bunny dream?" to which she replied, SMELL SOUND SOUND. *Omigawd*, I thought. It makes so much sense that the way she experiences dreams might not be as visual. Wouldn't her waking dominant senses play an important role in her dreamscape too? Wow, Bunny.

Not long after that, like a few days or something, Bunny approached the board and pressed RAIN. It was a bright and sunny day during a relentless summer heat wave. We'd experienced two this summer, with days on end of ninety-plus degrees, even some into the hundreds. No one in the Pacific Northwest has air-conditioning. It was brutal. And there was Bunny pressing RAIN. I said, "No. It's sunny. Today sunny. Do you want rain? I want rain too."

Bunny stood for a few moments, processing, then pressed RAIN MORE. "You want more rain? Me too, baby," I said. I thought that was the end of the conversation and stopped filming, but then she walked back to the board and pressed WATER DREAM. Could she have been dreaming of rain? Could dream mean to think? To remember?

Dreams are an incredibly important part of solidifying learned information. I have solved problems in dreams that I was incapable of doing during waking hours. I can only imagine the powerful insight we could gain through finding out more about the dreams of our pets. Keep dreaming, Buns, and I will too.

34

Not the Anxiety Again

I am Bunny, or Bunny is me—I don't even know anymore which of us is more like the other. Neither of us are completely stable—both of us are introverted and ruminate or perseverate with social anxiety, among the other anxieties, and reactive meltdowns, though mine are mostly inwardly directed. We're both funny, but not consistently so. More like a 70/30 awkward/funny split.

I've often wondered why a lot of dogs seem to share the personalities of their owners. Is it because people choose a dog that matches their disposition, or is it a trickle-down effect of owner lifestyle, temperament, and neuroses? Probably both. For sure both, right? In my case, given my near chronic anxiety, I often become more anxious imagining that Bunny's insecurities and reactivity are a direct result of mine. It makes me so sad. This is one of many reasons that I don't want human children. "Thanks for all the shit genetic predispositions,

Mom," I can just hear them saying. I s'pose I'll just have to avoid giving those words to Bunny.

Living and growing with Bunny has made me decidedly more intentional about monitoring my internal dialogue and autonomic nervous system. I always hated it when anyone would say "Take a deep breath." I wanted to shout, "You don't know what I need right now, let me just feel my damn feelings!" But now, having spent all this time coaching and supporting Bunny, I notice when I am experiencing my own tightness immediately, and I force myself to breathe.

I've been asked questions like, "If Bunny can talk, why not just modify her behavior with words? Have a conversation with her about it." And to some extent, I have. When I see Bunny barking angrily at a bird resting on our boat davit, I can ask her "Why mad?" and sometimes she'll respond BIRD or OUTSIDE LOOK or something like that, and it'll have been enough to take her out of the emotional arousal. In fact, birds don't have nearly the same emotional impact on her that they used to, and I imagine part of that is due to our repeated conversations surrounding them. But her level of concern surrounding birds is different than her level of concern surrounding, say, strangers in our house or an unknown dog invading her space. These cause an emotional state that seems more akin to panic. Brains work differently during panic. The amygdala (which helps process emotions) tells the hypothalamus (which regulates involuntary functions like breathing) that we're screwed. In response, the hypothalamus floods the autonomic nervous system with adrenaline and cortisol, preparing the body for fight or flight. Unnecessary functions in the body are turned off so as not to detract from the body's main goal: survival. One would think that with such hyperfocus on staying alive, a panic attack wouldn't feel quite so much like dying. At least that's what it feels like to me—not like I'm preparing for an epic battle. At any rate, the last thing Bunny wants to do when she's in this state is chat, and by the time she's out of the panic, chatting about it is still the last thing she wants to do. I've been almost entirely unsuccessful engaging Bunny in conversation about her reactivity. And I get it. Talking about big feelings like that is hard and scary, even for humans.

I really want to help Bunny through these challenges, so we work periodically with a couple of behavior consultants and behaviorists, one of whom recently came to our home. Bunny is reactive to strangers at our house, which in her case means that when someone that Bunny doesn't know well approaches our gate, comes onto the deck, or into our house, Bunny will bark loudly and aggressively, charge, and snap. This behavior didn't show up until she was just over a year old. We're a pretty introverted family as it is, but since we got her shortly before the COVID-19 pandemic began, that made socialization with strangers in our home challenging. Really, her only exposure to people in our home during that time was film crews and reporters wearing masks barreling into her space with large equipment. I didn't know any better at the time, and while I have since learned how to advocate for her and myself, thinking of those experiences and how they may have affected her makes me sad.

Anticipating Bunny's behavior and her anxiety leads to heightened anxiety in me when Johnny and I plan to have people over. It's not a lovely cycle. But when Kathy, our behavior consultant, came over, I was relaxed. I think it's because I knew with 100 percent certainty that she would know how to exist around a reactive dog. I wasn't afraid that she would try to pet Bunny, I could trust that she would ignore her, and that she could read her body language. The pressure was off of me, so I was able to relax. And guess what? Bunny didn't react. The consultant was in our home for a couple of hours, and although Bunny was tense, it was a night-and-day difference, which I attribute primarily to my own state of mind.

Kathy and I talked about how to mitigate my own anxiety prior to having guests over and established some training protocol that could help in the long run. Then, right after Kathy left, Bunny walked to her board and said, STRANGER YES MOM SETTLE YOU. Which I interpreted as something like, "A stranger was here but you were calm, Mom." Truths come out of the mouths of babes . . . and dogs.

35

Spicy Brain

You ever go to a Thai restaurant and think, *Yeah, I like spicy*, so you order three stars out of five and then after a few bites you're in another dimension, tongue numb, sweating through your pants, crying? Well, that's Buns. She's fucking spicy. I ordered two-star, but I got a ten-star spicy puppy. It's all good, mostly. Just always gotta have milk on hand, and by milk I mean fluoxetine, also known as doggy Prozac. I was blessed with spicy brain too, Buns. I get you.

Bunny lives by an exacting set of rules—mostly social, never linguistic—that only she knows. I try to follow the rules for her, but there are so many. The other night, I asked if she wanted to come up on the bed. She did. She hopped up, settled somewhat tensely beside me, and put her paw on my arm in what I interpreted as an act of affectionate solicitation. I gave her a few gentle scritches, testing the rule waters. She growled. I stopped immediately, removed my hand, and asked her, "Okay, Buns, what would you like me to do?" She peered earnestly at me and once again put her paw on my arm. This time

I chose to simply hold her paw and caress it gently, stopping every few seconds so that she could opt in again or opt out if she'd had enough. After a few reps of this, I paused, she growled, and I removed my hand again. It's so interesting how I've done all I can by giving her these words, really listening to her, and it's still hard to communicate sometimes. We don't even know what we need, I think. I've certainly struggled with that. "Well, now I'm super confused, Buns, I'm not sure what you want me to do here." She snorted indignantly and moved to the foot of the bed, a move I knew would become problematic because she had pinned a small corner of the sheet beneath her (just a couple inches really), and I needed it. As precise and delicate as a surgeon I slowly began to pull the sheet in my direction. Nothing gets past Bunny. She screamed, snapping air with the wild fervor of a starved alligator, then jumped off the bed and sulked into her crate. And this is Buns on meds.

Whatever the opposite of a foot fetish is, Bunny has that. Mostly it's human feet that bug her, although I did once see her growl at her own back paw after doing an involuntary kick. I think it's a sensory thing. Like they're too foreign and gross when they move but the rest of the human doesn't. If you're sitting near her and your foot moves in her direction, even an inch, she'll growl and storm off to the other side of the room. Dog forbid your foot actually touches her—she gets as mad about that as I've ever seen her about anything. It's kinda scary, but short-lived. A Cujo facade.

And don't get me started on the meltdowns at night, triggered by seemingly nothing, that could last hours. Barking, unable to settle, inconsolable. Eventually exhausting herself, she'll pass out but won't seem rested the next day. She'll have meltdowns during the day as well. She'll be triggered by seeing a stranger on the beach, and long after they're gone, she'll still be a wreck, barking, stiff-bodied with vigilance, staring out at the beach expecting the threat to reappear. One insult to her sensory landscape can send her reeling. An experience that I am not unfamiliar with, but have developed better coping skills for.

Well, better at pretending I'm coping, at least. But then, I've had forty years to practice.

Resource guarding? Yeah. We got that too. The day I brought her home as a teeny tiny puppy, she snarled and snapped at me for trying to take her bully stick (a popular dog chew that I later learned was made of bull pizzle). *All puppies do that*, I thought to myself. But I had a nagging suspicion that it might become a bigger issue. And it did. I worked hard in those early days on the issue, and she no longer guards from Johnny or me. But Otter better not eyeball her ducky. And of course, we're working on it.

In addition to anxious behavior, Bunny displays obsessive-compulsive, almost superstitious behavior, like licking the fireplace after every meal or walking a circle around her board before responding to a question. These traits combined with her sensory sensitivity led our behavior consultant to suggest that perhaps Bunny had canine autism, otherwise known as canine dysfunctional behavior—a label that I hate. It reminds me of how autism in humans was initially considered psychopathy. Like, we'll get there probably, but not without a few major bumps in the road. Not much is known about neurodivergence in dogs, and there isn't much research to pull from, which makes sense given how little we know about autism in humans. Coming to a diagnosis of autism in humans usually requires a series of self-assessment questionnaires or family-reported symptoms. Frequently these involve social communication and sensory responses. If the diagnosis fits . . .

I've been on various antidepressants or antianxiety medications since I was fourteen. I've tried them all. Basically, my brain just needs a little encouragement to keep itself from existential meltdown. Bunny, too, it seems. She was diagnosed with GAD, generalized anxiety disorder, at around one and a half years old. At that point in time, I didn't consider behavioral medication for her. She was an adolescent, still developing and under the influence of hormones and an assortment of genetic expressions, so it didn't seem appropriate. I was working with a couple of behavior consultants to help modify some of her most challenging behaviors, specifically her fear-based reactivity to dogs and strangers and her extreme sound sensitivity. But nothing was working as well as I would have hoped.

Now, I imagine some of you might be thinking that she is this way because I am this way. I thought this, too, at one point. That I might have a slow leak of anxiety, depression, and insecurity that oozes out of my palms and is absorbed by Bunny when I scritch behind her ears. I was delighted and relieved to learn that this is not the case, having been reassured by many behavior consultants, and then re-reassured by them when I unfailingly ask, "But are you sure?" Dogs can smell serotonin and cortisol, so they surely are quite capable of determining our moods, but what they do with that information is unique to the individual animal. While she may of course be influenced by my behavior, she doesn't just absorb my maladies. This point is reinforced by Otter's unyielding good nature. He's the fun guy. He is the friend that you want with you at parties when you're the introvert. He rolls with the punches and generally just enjoys most things. "Perpetually down to clown," as they say (not sure who "they" are, but I do appreciate this idiom). These are not qualities that he has absorbed from me. I am decidedly *not* the fun guy. I mean, I used to be when my social superpower was substances, but that's not really me, if you know what I mean. I'm not boring or anything, but I'd rather be home.

We can debate all day what the cause of "disordered" behavior might be, but we can also just respect that it is the magic and mystery of genetics. Bunny's genetics set her up for extraordinary sensitivity, which is reflected in all the ways she communicates. And it makes navigating the unpredictability of daily life more challenging.

So when Bunny was about two and a half, and with the help of our behavior consultant and our vet, we decided to give fluoxetine a shot. If you've ever been depressed or severely anxious, then you'll understand that when you're in that state, you can't do much. Everything besides simply getting through the day is a side note. You can't think. How can we expect ourselves or an animal to effectively change behavior when just existing is a challenge?

It takes a while for a drug like fluoxetine to take effect, but around the one-month mark, I began to notice what I can only describe as a softening of Bunny's behavior. Reactions still occurred, but her recovery time was shorter. I was able to talk her off the ledge now. And because she wasn't constantly in autonomic panic, we could effectively implement some alternative coping strategies.

I'd tried giving Bunny pills before, pain meds after her spay. It wasn't easy. She doesn't like pill pockets, doesn't like peanut butter, is super particular about cheese, doesn't care for marshmallows. So I knew we'd need a long-term solution if she was going to be taking daily medication. The first thing I tried was hiding the pill from her and wrapping it in deli meat. She'd quickly evict the pill from its meaty packaging with surgical precision, spit it on the floor, give me a disgusted look, then walk away. After a while she just refused the meat altogether. Since I'd seemingly poisoned the thought of Black Forest ham for her, I adopted a different tactic. New meat, who this, and also I started telling her what we were doing and why. Narrating the process using words she was familiar with added predictability. Just like me, Bunny is excellent at pattern recognition and appreciates knowing what to expect. I added a medicine button. Every morning I'd press the button and say, "Okay, Bunny, let's do medicine." Then I'd show her the pill, and as I wrapped it in our new meat (prosciutto) I'd say, "This is for all done sad, all done concerned." As though what she'd needed all along was simply an honest explanation of what was about to happen, giving her back a tiny bit of control. I resonate so deeply with this that I felt sad about not having thought of it sooner.

My sadness was short-lived as I began to realize that Bunny, too, recognized the value of her morning medicine. I mean, it literally sounds crazy, but one morning while Johnny was gone for a couple of weeks over the summer, Bunny approached her board and said SMALL CONCERNED CONCERNED. "I'm sorry. Why small concerned?" I asked. SAD BIG, Bunny replied. "Why? Because Dad bye? Are you big sad because Dad bye?" I continued. DO MEDICINE, Bunny replied. Had I heard that right? Had I interpreted it right? Was I overinterpreting? She trotted after me into the kitchen and happily took her medicine.

One morning a couple of weeks later, I was prepping Bunny and Otter for my departure. I was headed out to run some errands and I told them I was leaving but that I'd be back a little bit later. Bunny looked thoughtful, so I asked her what was on her mind. FORGET REMEMBER BEFORE MORNING MEDICINE, she said. I was gobsmacked and stumbled over my words, saying, "I . . . did I forget morning . . . I did forget morning medicine!"

Behavior medications aren't a magic bullet, but they give us enough emotional space between a trigger and a reaction that we can find coping mechanisms in between. They allow us to learn. We can finally breathe. And for as much as I can't stand when someone tells *me* to breathe, I put it on cue for Bunny. You can train a dog to take deep breaths. And just like for us, that focus on breath and influx of oxygen can help to reset their sympathetic nervous system. As I cue Bunny to breathe, modeling the breaths myself, I realize that I've been sweetly tricked into doing what's best for myself by doing what's best for someone else.

36

Where Do We Go from Here?

Bunny has been in my life for a little over three years at the time of this writing. It feels like the blink of an eye, but we've been busy. We've been in the *New York Times*, the *Wall Street Journal*, and *Vice*. We've been on Netflix, and Bunny is the first nonhuman ever to be on a *Forbes* list. I've achieved my personal goal of exemplary connection and communication with Bunny and now have started that adventure with Otter as well.

I think year three with a dog is my favorite so far. I hope it continues this way, with each year topping the last. I imagine it will. Watching Bunny and Otter evolve is one of the most fun and fulfilling experiences of my life—the more I learn about them, the more I adore them. Bunny has matured and I'm starting to see aspects of personality really solidify. She's still a serious girl who

takes no shit. She's sensitive and sweet, not particularly biddable. Definitely a scaredy-cat although she'd never admit it. One of the more charming attributes I've noticed in her since the puppy and adolescent energy has quelled (because I can relate) is that she's an absolute leisure pony. She'd choose to stay in a sun puddle on the couch all day if she could. She's basically a cat . . . or a philosophical houseplant. But for real, she'll turn down walks until I basically have to lecture her about the importance of exercise. She'll roll her eyes and reluctantly stick her neck out so that I can get a collar on her. Then she'll walk with a mission: head down, brisk pace, like "Let's get this over with." I love her so much. But after the walk, she's so happy we went, she'll do figure eights around my legs with a huge smile and tiny roos. Like going to the gym. I never want to go, and I'm miserable while I'm there, but I'm so glad I went once I'm back to the safety and comfort of my couch.

All these delightful qualities are made more obvious by the stark contrast in Otter's equally charming character. He's fully in adolescence right now and it feels like he changes daily. But there's a really beautiful through line of easygoing, sweet boy, with a dash of himbo jock. He's an athlete and an immediate *yes* to any and all activity (as long as it involves me). He's a go-anywhere guy and loves to work. He also enjoys a good snuggle, which I can't get enough of. He and I are exploring all sorts of sports. He's titled in Dash and Precision Coursing, has a few trick titles, a conformational grand championship, and we're learning Rally Obedience and Agility. He and Bunny couldn't be more different, and together they continue to challenge my assumptions about what is normal and engage me in metaphorical and occasionally literal conversations around radical acceptance.

When I started exploring AAC three years ago, there were only a handful of people doing this work with dogs. Of all the changes the last few years have brought, the number of pet guardians embracing what we now call AIC (augmentative interspecies communication) and the number of teams exploring the

depths of connection and communication like us might be the most dramatic shift I've seen. It has been a relief to have more people advocate for the potential these devices have for deepening understanding between humans and their animal companions. I feel like I can take my foot off the gas a little bit. To be honest, it's a welcome change for a few reasons. One is that the older Bunny and Otter get, the less I feel compelled to use the buttons as a tool to communicate with them. Don't get me wrong, the buttons were a huge reason I got to know Bunny as well as I did when I was first getting to know her. But now, a few years in, I feel like I know them well enough to listen to what they're telling me without them having to say it all the time. Sometimes words get in the way, but often enough Bunny will use AIC to communicate something I couldn't otherwise have known, and I find myself thankful to have a floor covered in talking buttons.

That's what a lot of people are getting out of AIC. It's not that their animals are finally communicating—we always knew they were communicating. It's that we've found this tool that acts as a catalyst to get us to listen more closely to what they're saying, and now we can do that without the buttons. The act of putting my intention toward listening to my dog forced me to learn about a lot of things that make listening easier because I began to understand what I was hearing. Hearing Bunny speak to me in English was what truly inspired me to learn Dog, and our need for buttons has diminished as we start to just get each other as two animals in the room. I certainly don't claim to know what all the ethical implications might be surrounding teaching Bunny to communicate in this way, but I do know that when you put connection first, and put as much effort into understanding those around you as you do into trying to be understood, the impetus to communicate flourishes.

Even in this, the final chapter of my book, I struggle to perfectly encapsulate all that I've learned and how I've grown with Bunny and within myself over the last three years. Because this isn't the final chapter. This is really just the beginning. We have so much more to learn and share. So much more to explore within connection and communication. Once you start really listening, worlds become accessible that are not limited by language or species, politics or religion. A greater empathy unfolds that changes not only how we communicate with nonhumans, but with our fellow humans as well. I am endlessly honored to care for Bunny and Otter, whose lessons I couldn't have learned anywhere else, and who have made me an undeniably better human.

I'd like to specifically thank several people and generally thank a whole lot more.

During my time as a designer, I was lucky enough to collaborate with a slew of incredibly talented photographers, makeup artists, and hair stylists. Several of them became close friends. Six of them—all brilliant, strong women (and one man)—created with me the photographic art that you see in this book. That chapter of my life ended somewhat abruptly, so to be able to bring it full circle here feels like a gift. These people are photographer Elle Hanley (ellehanley.com); photographer Amanda Calquhoun; photographer Rhiannon Brunett, Thisisrhi Photography; photographer Vera Pashkevich (verapashphoto.com); makeup artist Codee Bradley; hair stylist Paige Craft; and Lance Reis (lancereis.com). This book is richer because of each of your contributions, as is my life.

Big thanks to Agata Zlotko (agatazlotko.com) for the most perfect illustrations. I can't wait until we are in the same country at the same time and you can finally tattoo your artwork on me.

I'd like to thank Johnny for remaining levelheaded every time I swear I'm going to do the impossible against all odds. I think he thinks I'm capable of everything, and that's a really nice space to live in.

And to my parents, I couldn't be more grateful that you love Bunny as much as I do and that she lights up every time she hears

ACKNOWLEDGMENTS

your names. Knowing that our sweet, sensitive girl has a secondary safe haven with you brings me so much comfort.

Thank you to my therapist Kathleen and my Dog Behavior Consultant mentor (just a different type of therapist really) Sarah Richter.

Thank you, HarperCollins, for trusting me to write a book worth reading. Thank you to my manager, Charley; to my editor, Andrew; to my literary agent, Ryan; and to FluentPet.

And thank you to every single follower for staying curious and open, and for allowing me to share all that I've learned with you. I can't wait to see where we go next.

ABOUT THE AUTHOR

Alexis Devine is an artist and entrepreneur hailing from Seattle, Washington. She was a longtime creator of wearable art before her sheepadoodle Bunny, known as "What About Bunny" on social media, became an internet sensation in the fall of 2020. Videos of her communicating with assistive technology from FluentPet went viral. Bunny now has over one hundred buttons individually programmed with various words that she uses to communicate how she feels, what she wants, to express when she is in pain, and even to chat about her dreams. She is part of an ongoing canine cognition research study at the Comparative Cognition Lab at UCSD. They have recently added a standard Poodle to the family named Otter whom Alexis is training with the same system. These days Alexis is a Licensed Family Dog Mediator, Fear Free Certified Professional, and Certified Canine Enrichment Technician. Her goal is to further our understanding of the power of connection and importance of empathy, meeting her dogs where they are and understanding them on their terms first to facilitate trust and promote an environment that supports them as the incredible creatures they are.